ABANDONED SOUTH AUSTRALIA

AN ARID JOURNEY

SHANE THOMS

AUSTRALIA THROUGH TIME

The creators of this book's content fully acknowledge and recognise the Traditional Custodians of the land on which these structures were built and pay our respects to all elders past, present, and emerging. Although this publication does not deeply explore the Indigenous stories of the spaces explored, the creators of its content recognise that Australia's First Nations people have occupied and cared for this continent for over 65,000 years. And no matter where we are across this nation, Australia always was and always will be Aboriginal and Torres Strait Islander land.

Australia Through Time
is an imprint jointly owned by

Woodslane Press Pty Ltd, 10 Apollo Street, Warriewood, NSW 2102, Australia
Email: info@woodslane.com.au
Tel: 02 8445 2300
Website: woodslanepress.com.au

and

Fonthill Media, Millview, Toadsmoor Road, Stroud, GL5 2TB, United Kingdom
Tel: 01453 886959
Website: www.fonthill.media

First published in Australia in 2022 by Fonthill Media and Woodslane Press, reprinted 2025

NATIONAL LIBRARY OF AUSTRALIA
A catalogue record for this book is available from the National Library of Australia

MIX
Paper | Supporting responsible forestry
FSC www.fsc.org FSC® C006474

Printed in China by SC (Sang Choy) International Pte Ltd

WOODSLANE PRESS

FONTHILL

CONTENTS

Thanks to my friend Kat Hayes and my family

INTRODUCTION

ABANDONED SOUTH AUSTRALIA

This book tells a ghost story. Or, scores of them.

The spaces within this book feel ghostly. Standing within a building heavy with thick swathes of dust, furnished with chairs left in positions once choreographed, or encroached by tendrils of nature trying to creep into corners, you can almost feel the ghosts blowing on the back of your neck. These spaces are dormant, but some still feel alive. It does not take much imagination to see beyond the dust, to the occupants who once sat on the chairs, to the windows and walls sealing in warmth and life. The ghosts want you to know they are there—things creak and eeriness enshrouds.

But the myth of *terra nullius* is the real lingering ghost of the abandoned spaces of Australia. These spaces, in South Australia, always were and always will be the land of many Indigenous groups, dating back over 40,000 years: from the Peramangk and Kaurna people to the south of the state, Adnyamathanha and Dieri to the east, up north Antakirinja land, and the western Kokatha people—and many more. The abandoned spaces within this book were constructed on an ancient land that existed long before the colonial cement was poured.

When observing this ancient land's timeline, the abandoned houses, farms, schools, or any one of the derelict post-colonial establishments in South Australia are merely finite remnants of the most recent occupants of South Australia's spaces.

Formerly a land with copper in its ground, once a bounteous plain of wine grapes and wheat, previously also home to a nuclear bomb testing site and—like all of Australia—rich with Indigenous past, South Australia's history is long, complex, and unable to be summed up in this book's introduction; and the spaces within this book are mere fragments of a history that deserves to be told.

But here, images of these fragments make for small albeit potent vignettes. South Australia, now, has abandoned spaces that dot its landscape with stories halted and ghosts active. South Australia boasts these places frozen in time: sketches of farmers and animals; women and men; parents and children.

The longevity of humanity extends. We live on through pestilence and fire, plague and flood. We sleep through war and wind, each morning stretching our shoulders and shrugging off the inescapable feeling of cyclical inevitability pressing down upon them. The ruins of past iterations of us, weary folk facing another day in a routine that will one day be broken, are left behind. Those people stretched, one day, for the last time in a bed now abandoned in a town 600 kilometres north of Adelaide.

We underscore our own obsession with mortality by revisiting these spaces, by seeking them out and reconstructing animation where there is none. We attach our own identities to those who walked and stretched and slept before us. We are confronted by the end of things, yet frozen in our own scenes. We are waiting in the wings of our own future, ready to make our entrance.

The ruins of South Australia are barren, isolated time capsules. Silence permeates. A stark contrast to Adelaide's busy city centre, the abandoned realm reminds us of its ghostly origins by the stillness of its places, light streaming through dust and wind fluttering between dead leaves. Time is relative here: how long will this building stand, and how long has it? Will it be knocked down to make room for newer, dustless blocks? We pause and consider the streams of dust that will be disturbed, breaking the calmly steady encompassment they have had with plaster, joinery, wood carvings, and intricate tiling. And before the bulldozers arrive, the light streams in and illuminates memory along with the dust.

The ghosts will run when the disassembly begins, seeking out new places to hover, bidding their former homes farewell. The sweet decay that fed them banished, these ghosts have no place to linger within the shiny shells of modern constructions.

And so, as the audience, we look and wonder. Which ghosts were resident in these houses of yore, these farms of the past now ground to a halt? Who loved and lived, briefly, through existences that unfolded one day into the dusty ground?

We see, in the grimy windows and arid yards, echoes of our own impermanence, traces of family homes and share-houses we have lived in before and never truly known. Another 365 sleeps in a place that functioned as a stepping stone to where the former occupants are now. A place to deliver our own mortality—time continues, but we will not. We pay our respects to the past and present elders of ancient land, and we wonder who its guests were in the meantime.

Political or economic instabilities are not the only reasons to turn to when we ask, why are these buildings abandoned? Factories, schools, mines, houses, hospitals, and other buildings all over the country have been left to decay for a number of different reasons, with the exploration of each space revealing some part of what is its own unique—and new—story.

We may never know why these farmhouses, schools, and stations were left, and we will never know who switched off the lights for the last time. Perhaps they will not know themselves. We do know that these places contrast the past, present, and future, invoking necessary discussions about land and space that should always be present in our throats. All we can do is fictionalise the stories of those who came to live and dwell. *Abandoned South Australia* looks to the clues of the post-colonial buildings themselves to capture pockets of time of inhabitancy. The stories here are mere portions of the long histories of Australia's abandoned spaces.

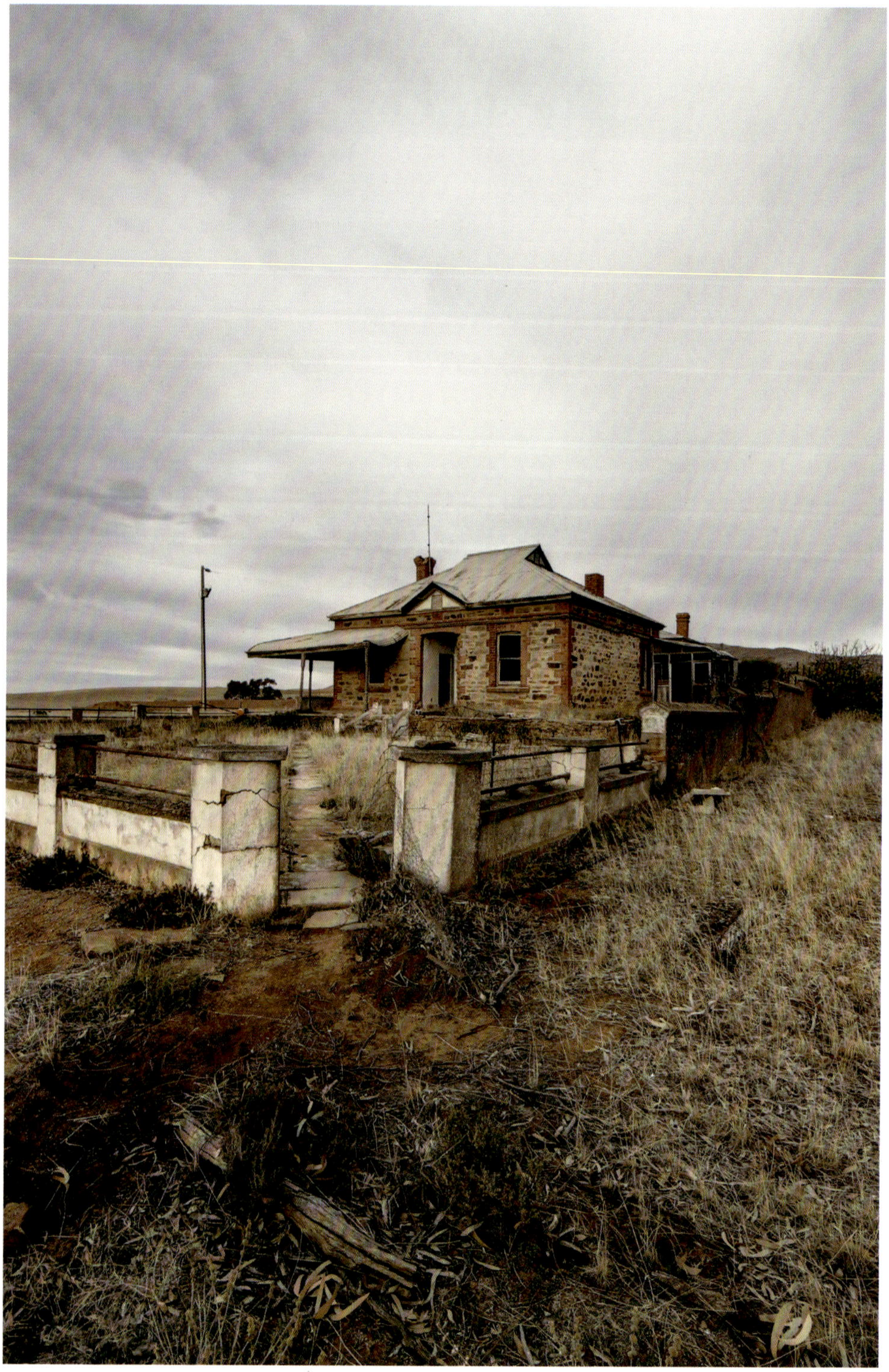

1

FARMHOUSES

The sandstone buildings left to decay in the farming regions of South Australia mirror the very substance they are created from: dry, red, or tan-coloured establishments built by blocks made from hard rural land and desert. These tiny tundras make up structures that remain abandoned, left to decay due to a failed attempt at farming, a newer house on the property or the pursuit of a busier life somewhere else. Sandstone is an important part of the region's architectural heritage, and these blocks of sedimentary rock tell us stories of those long gone.

Members of rural farming families that once lived lively existences of motion and noise, the tiny desert blocks housing rich, fertile actualities of people and their loved ones. One can almost smell the smoke of fires that were kept burning all day and night, and hear the creak of rocking chairs that sat before them, holding weary bones. Water tanks stand as silent and rusting sentinels as if to watch over the ruins next to them. Once providing necessary life, now dry and lifeless.

Later, some of these original farmhouses were repurposed: used as horse tack rooms, storage spaces for agricultural tools, a room relegated for just one purpose rather than utilised as a dynamic family space. But many were not repurposed, and these are what we see before us: four-walled time capsules, often featuring original furnishings and objects discarded by sheep shearers, horse racers, dairy farmers, cattle herders. Spaces where mothers, fathers, aunts, sons all worked and lived and slept and ate.

Yellow smoke-stained walls and pastel pressed tin ceilings echo the domestic stories of the past where the smoke from stoves, fires and pipes, once so potent, still lingers. Picturing the bathing and ablution rituals of the past is easy, as porcelain basins and bathtubs are often still intact. And the ghosts of the inhabitants' personal treasures—but perhaps those not treasured enough to take with them—remain. Wardrobes and other furniture are sometimes still full of original clothing and shoes that once wrapped themselves around feet long gone.

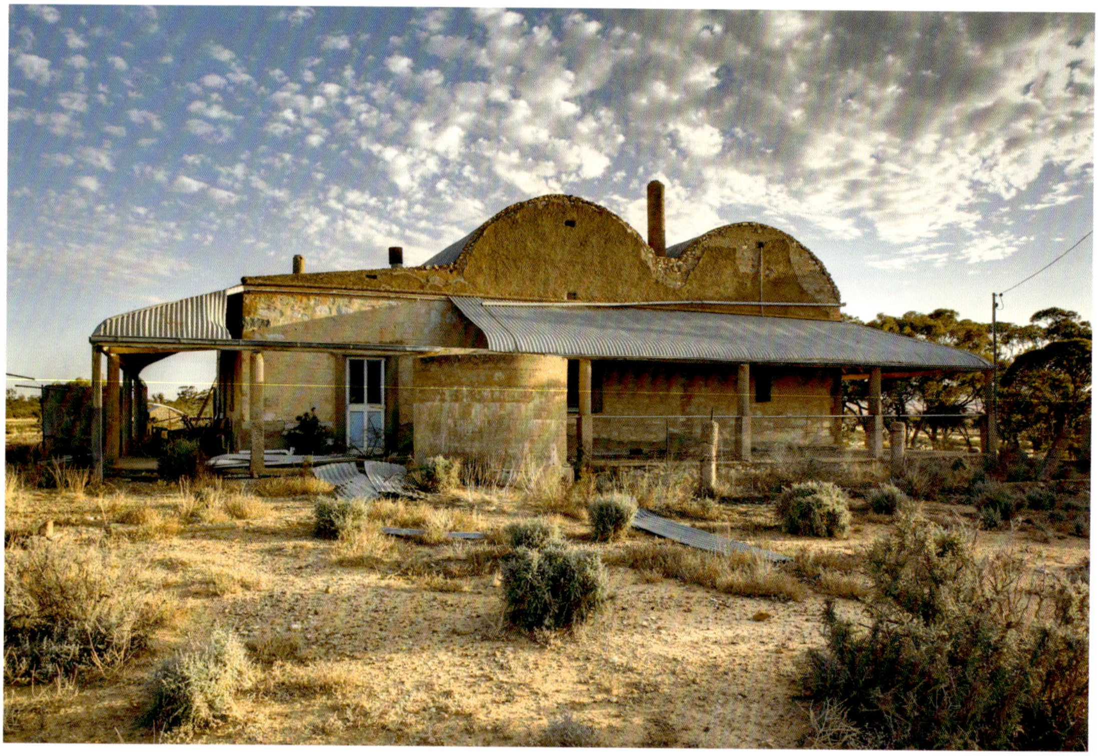

A unique abandoned farmhouse with an uncharacteristic domed roof.

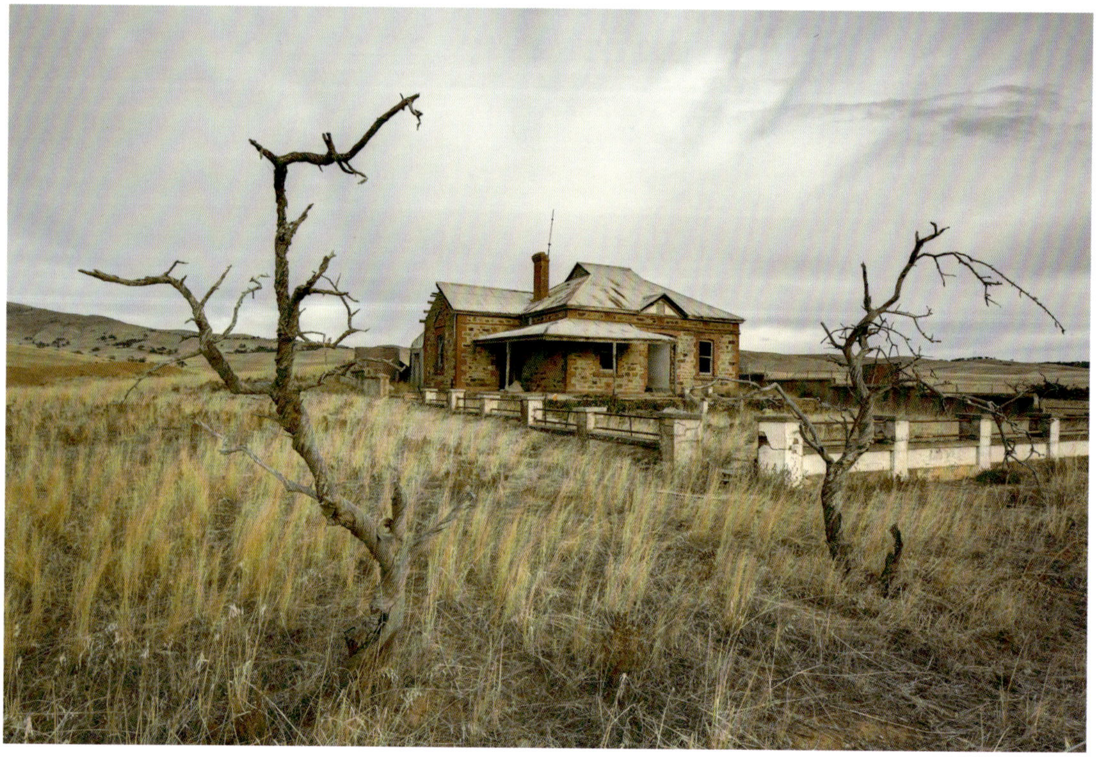

A derelict cottage in South Australia's north-eastern corner.

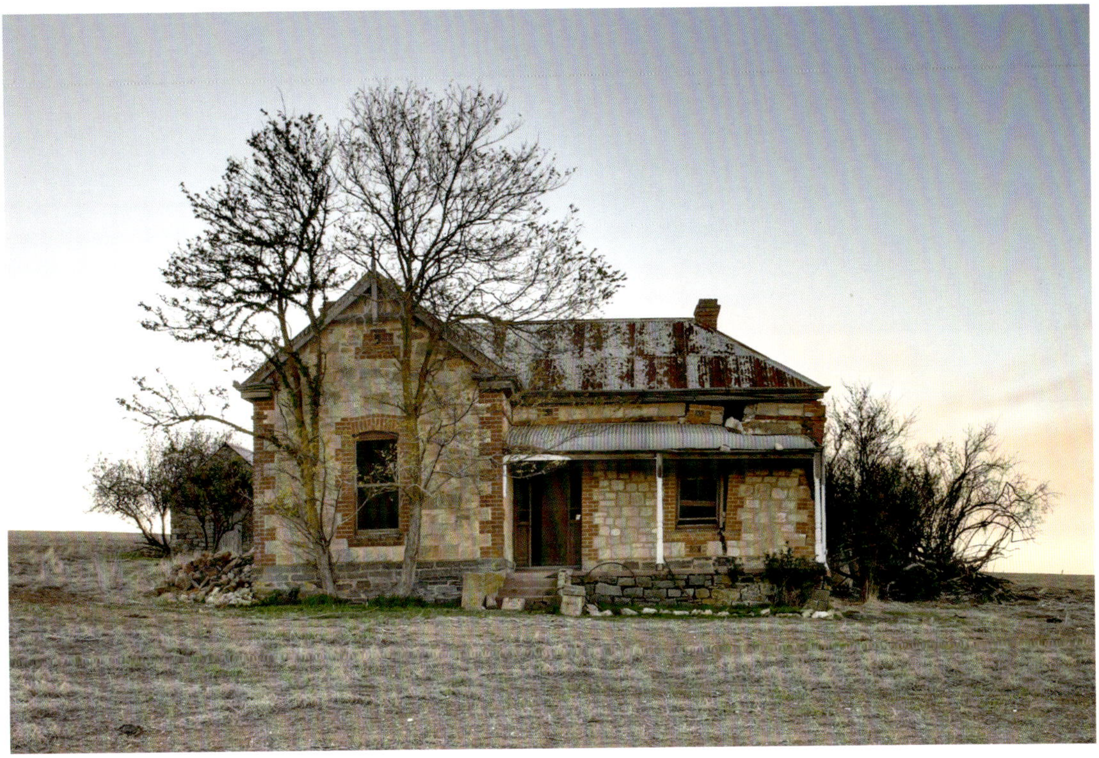

A typical period stone homestead.

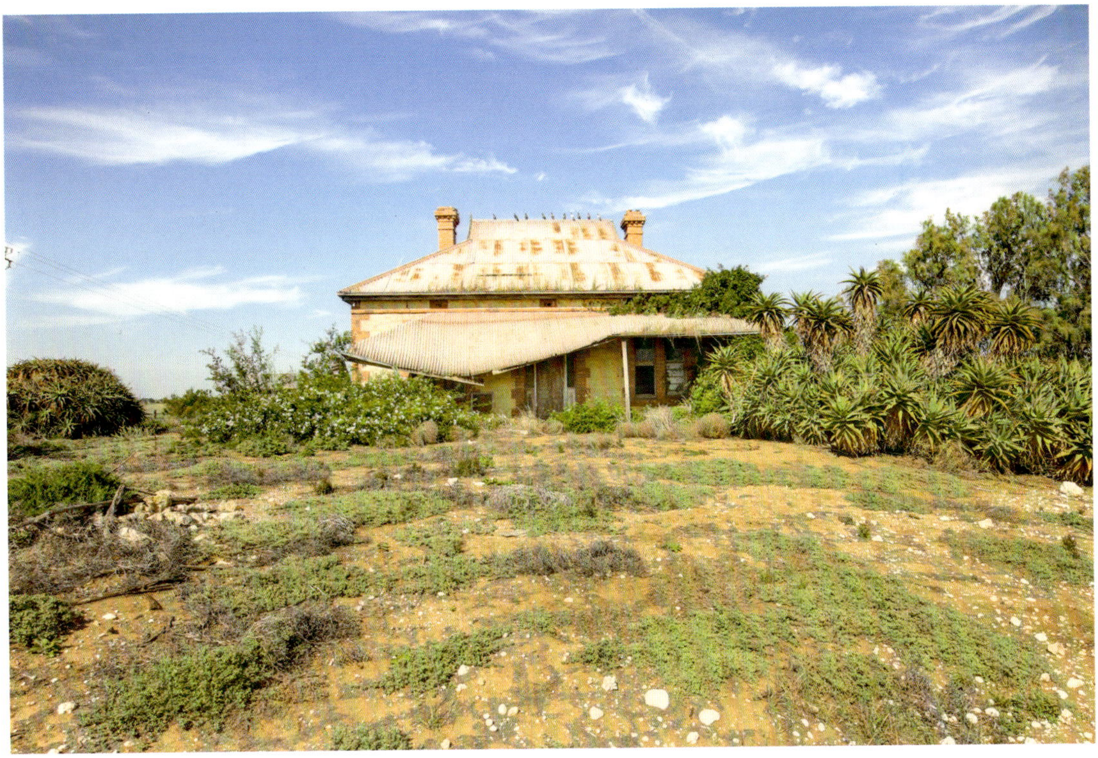

Each year, the overgrowth and shrubs edge closer to this quaint stone farmhouse located near the township of Murray Bridge.

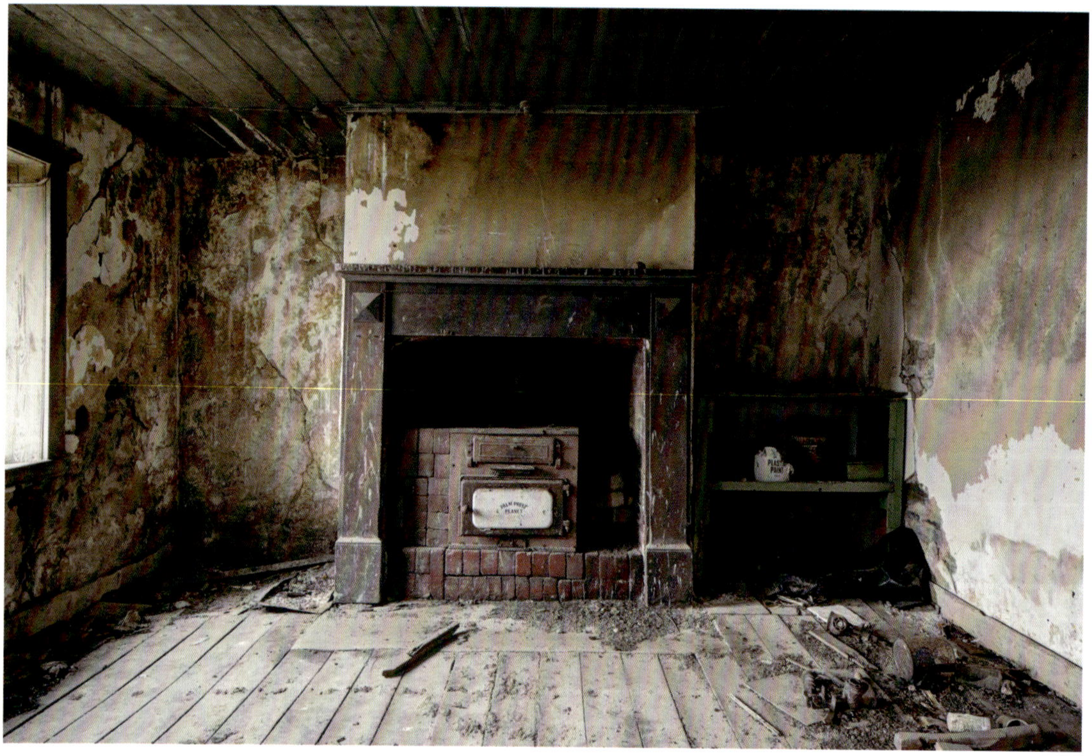

A kitchen interior with its original wood-fire stove.

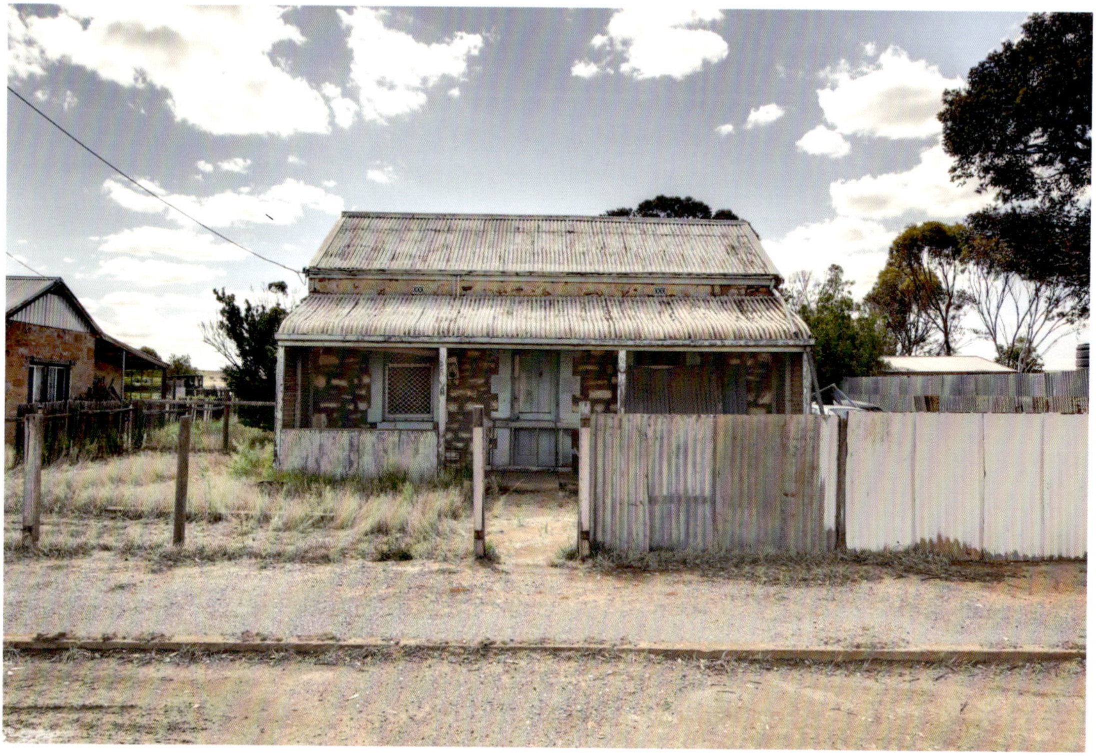

Human bones were discovered inside the fireplace of this abandoned house located in a quiet Mid-Northern township.

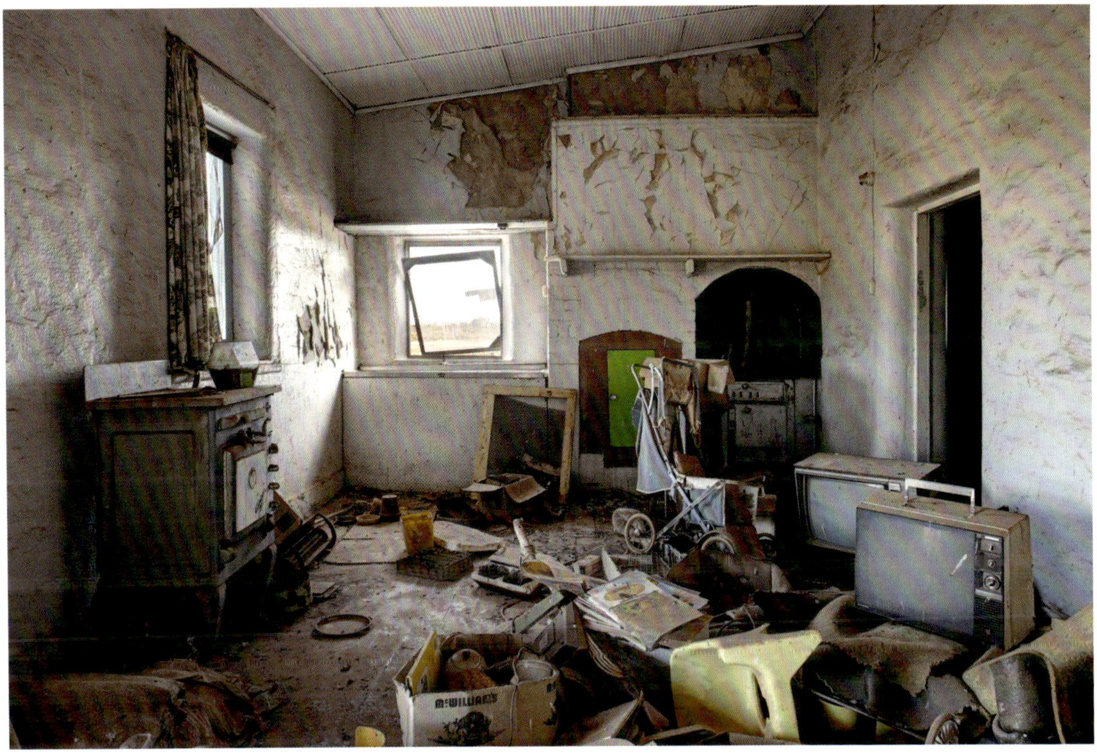

Discarded household items left behind in a country dwelling.

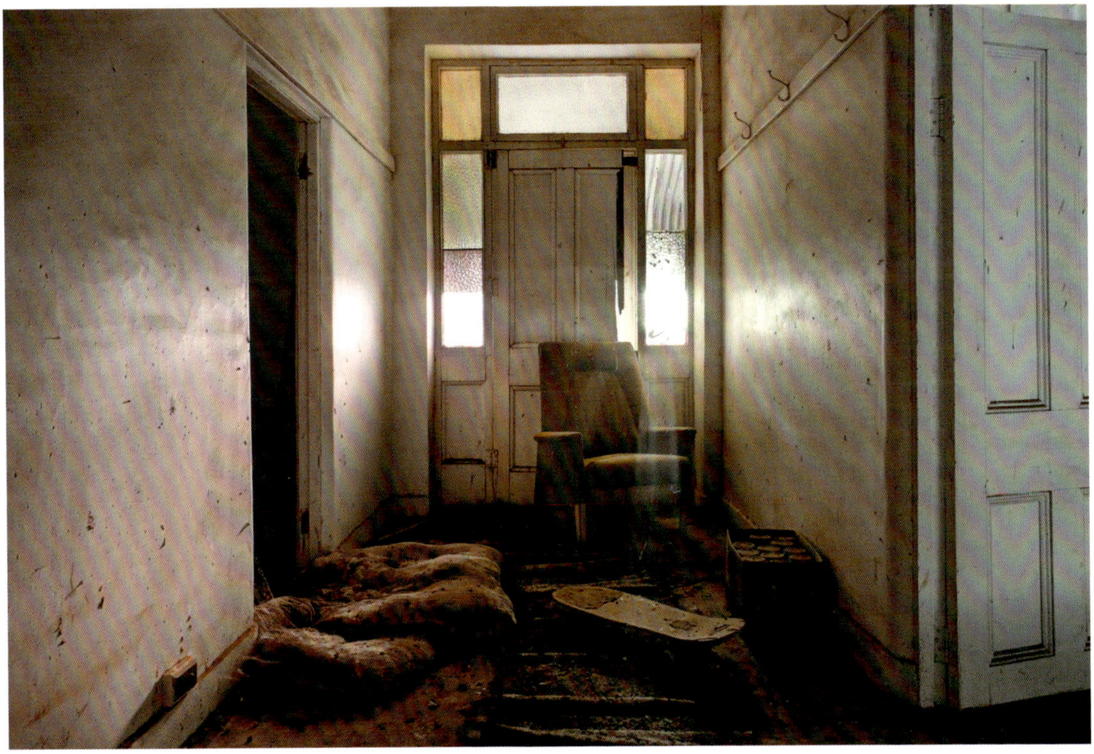

The dust-filled hallway of a forgotten period home.

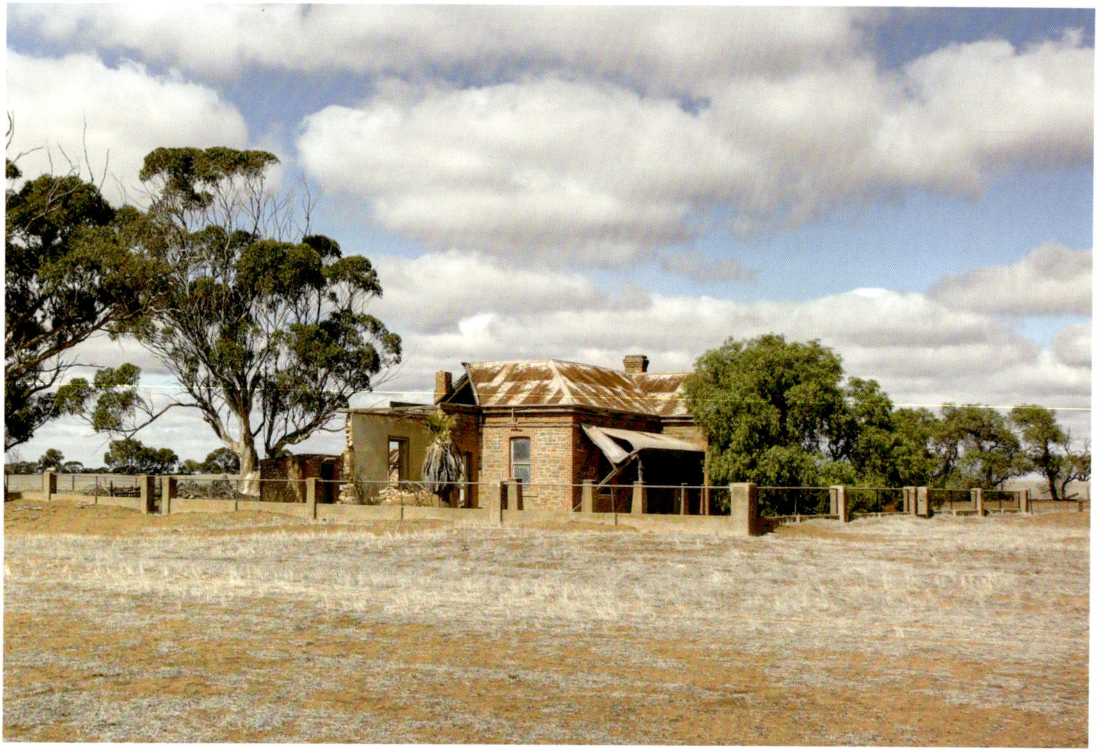

A typical farmhouse ruin.

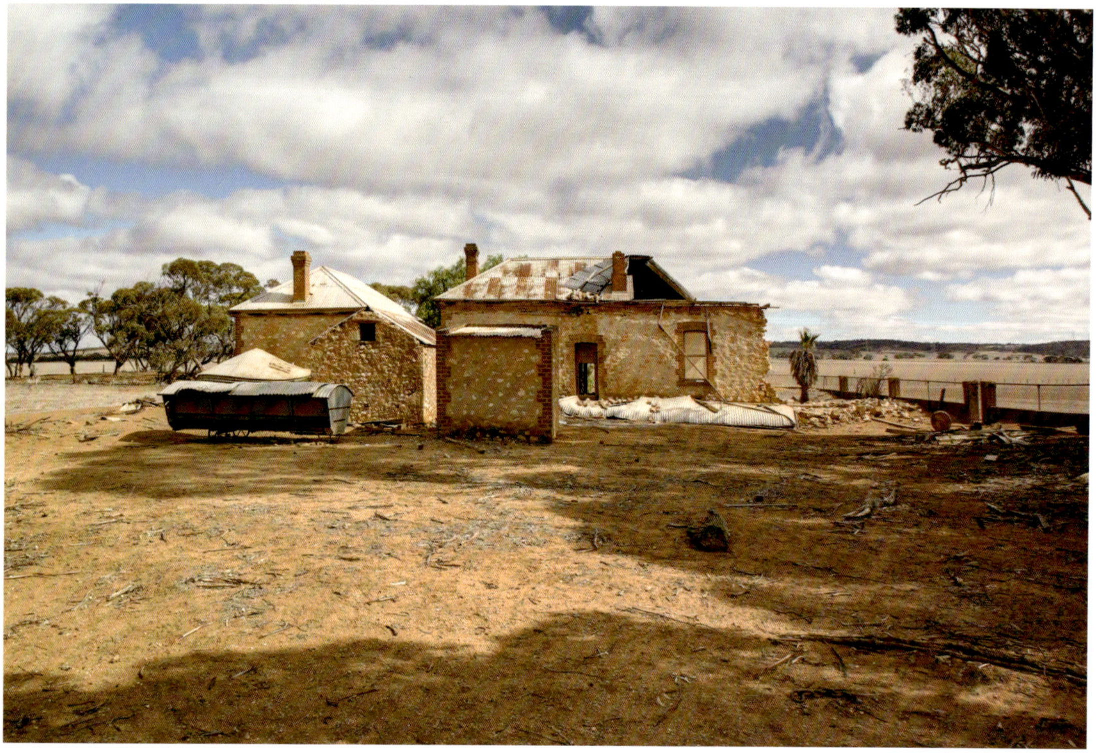

The rear of a crumbling homestead.

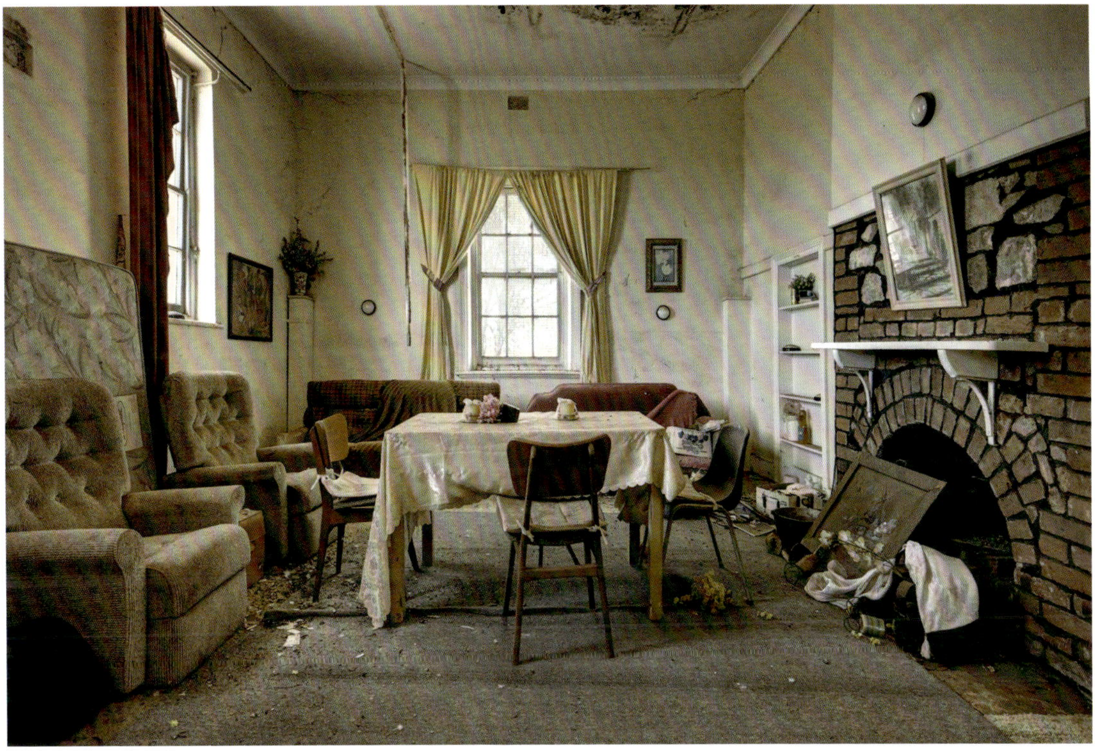

A furnished lounge room interior in a country farmhouse.

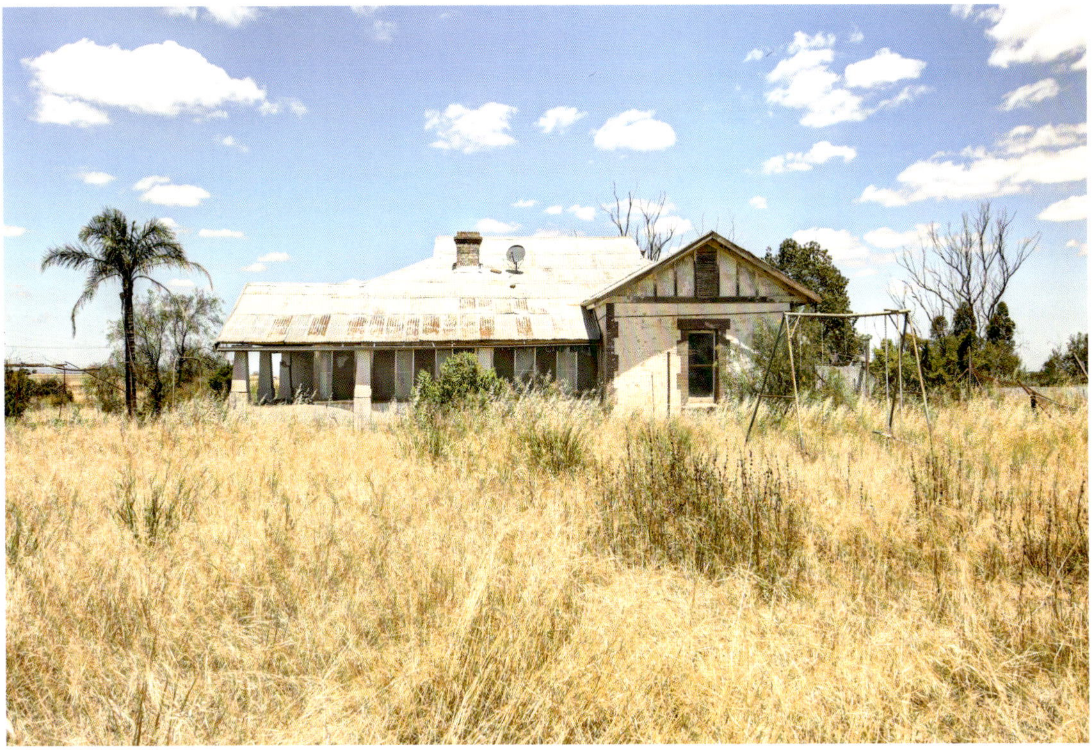

A farmhouse sits forgotten in a rural area near Hamley Bridge.

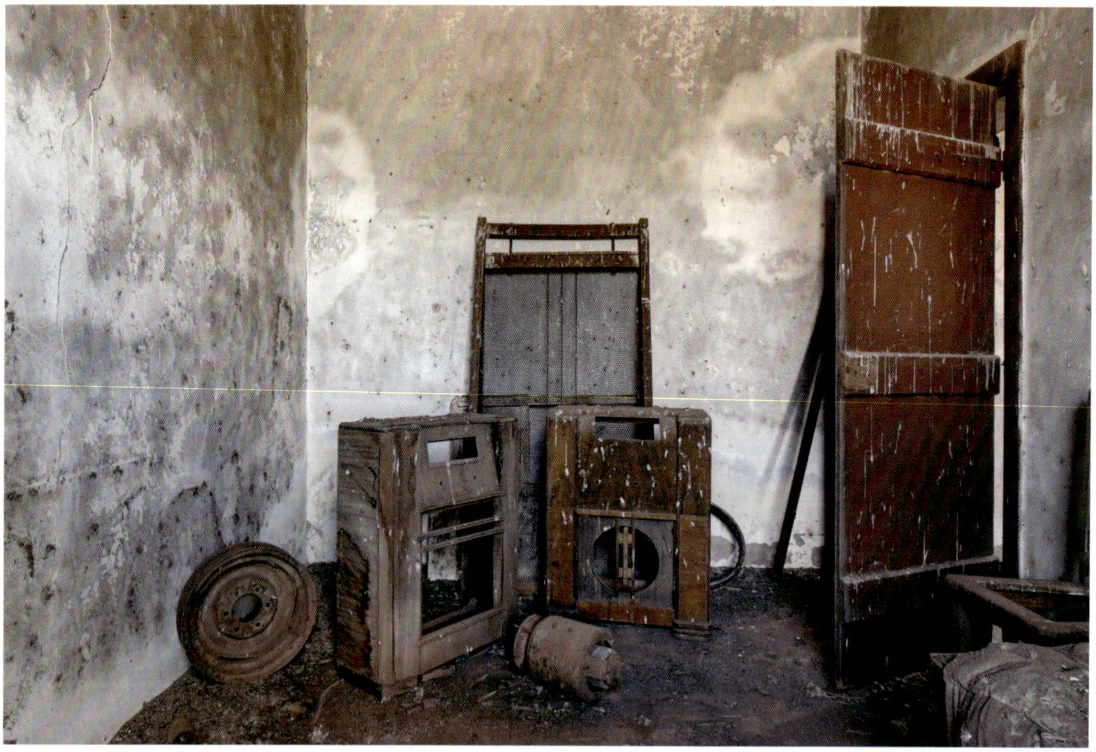

The shells of two wooden console radios.

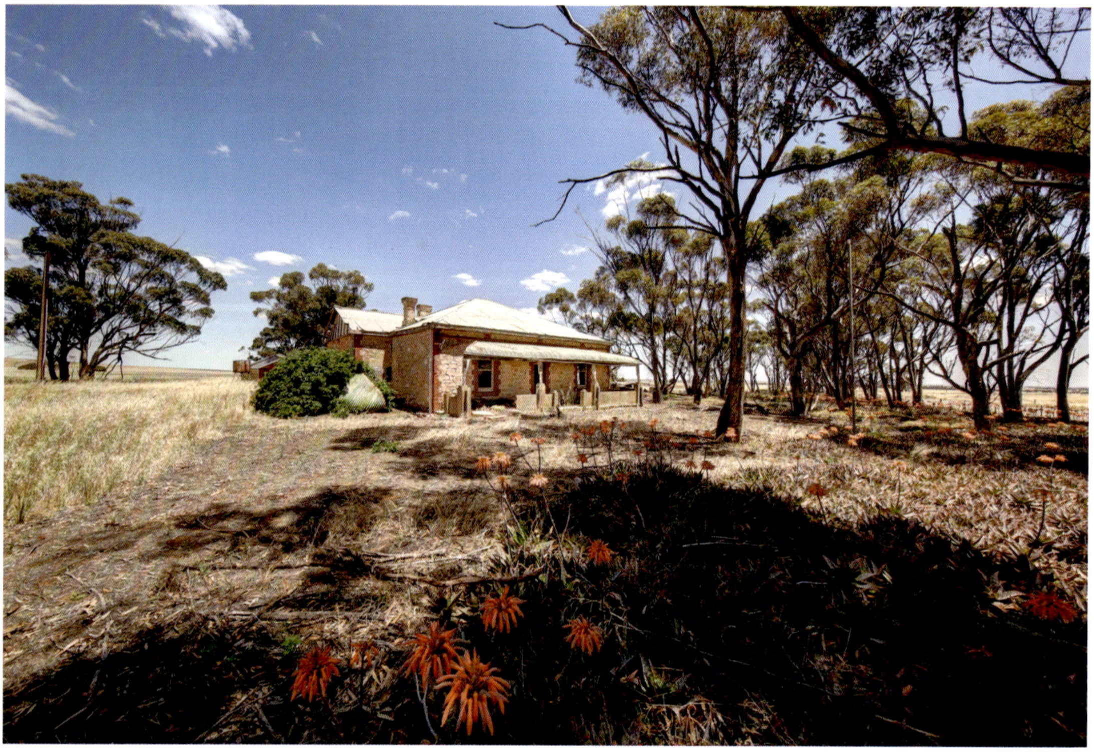

An abandoned homestead in the Alma region.

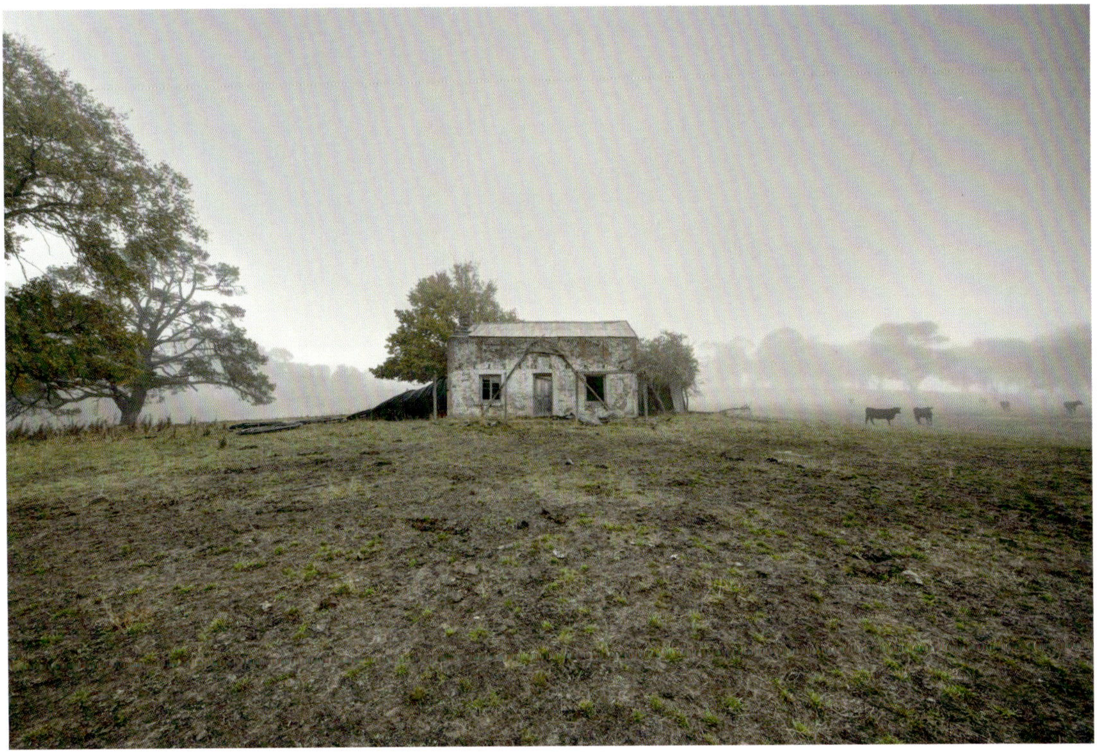

A simple four-walled stone farm cottage now used as storage space.

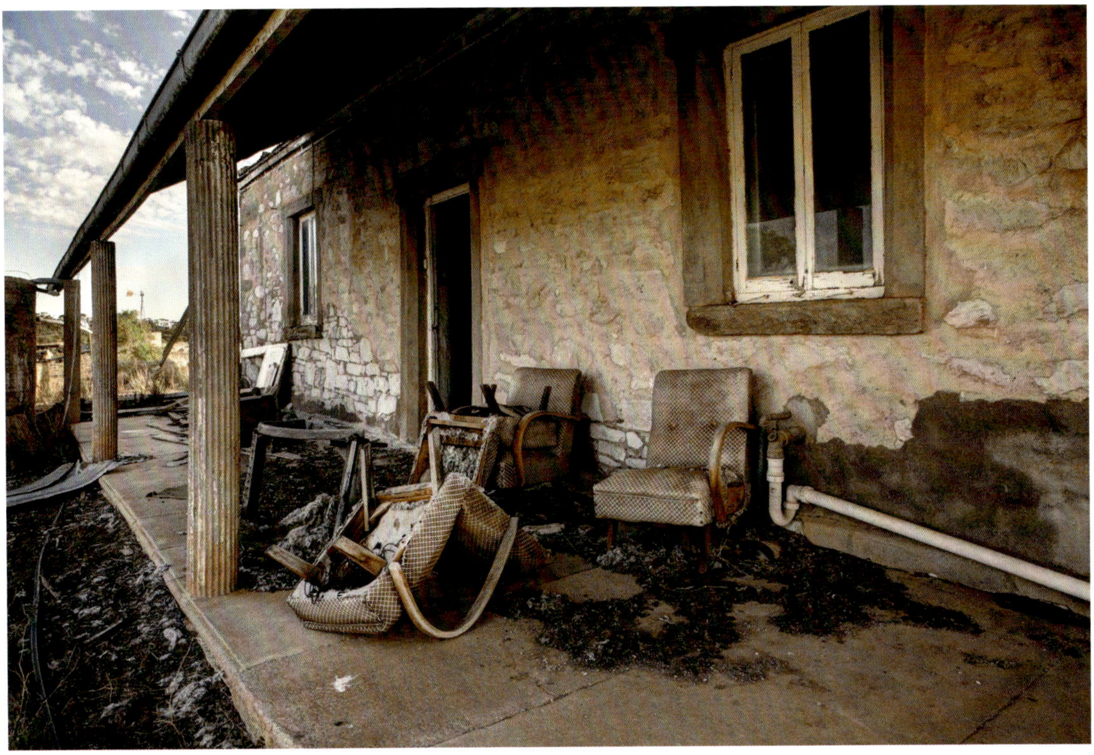

A back porch facing the morning horizon.

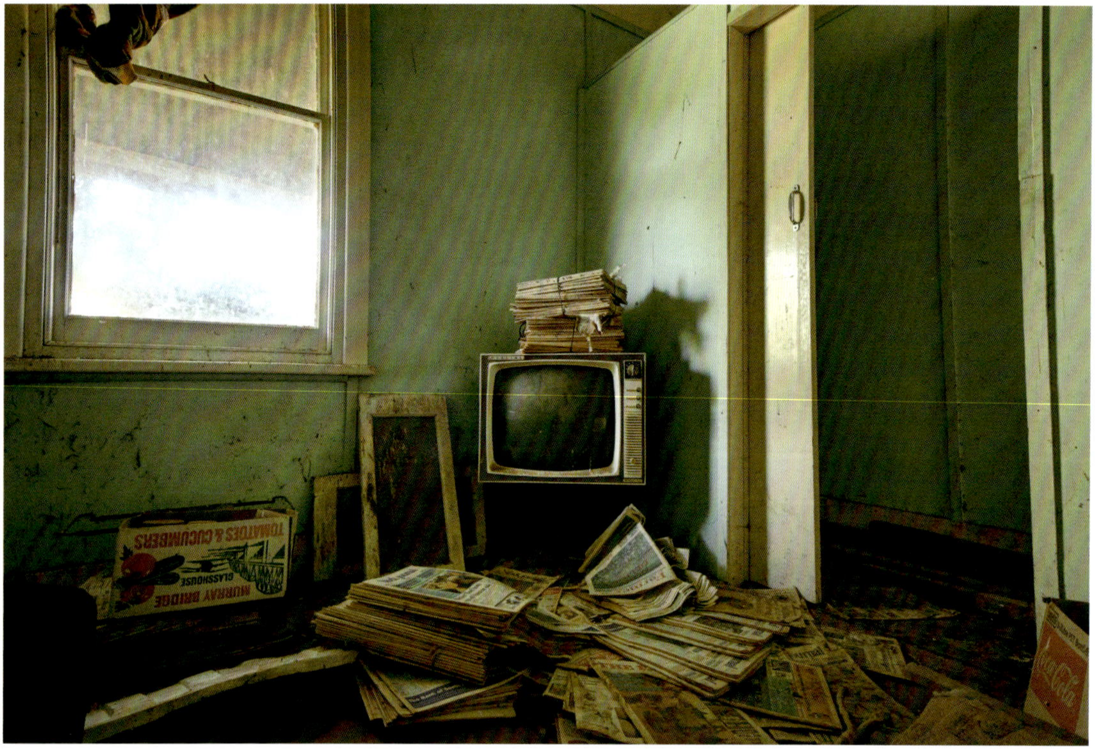

Decades-old newspapers lay scattered inside this dust-filled former bedroom.

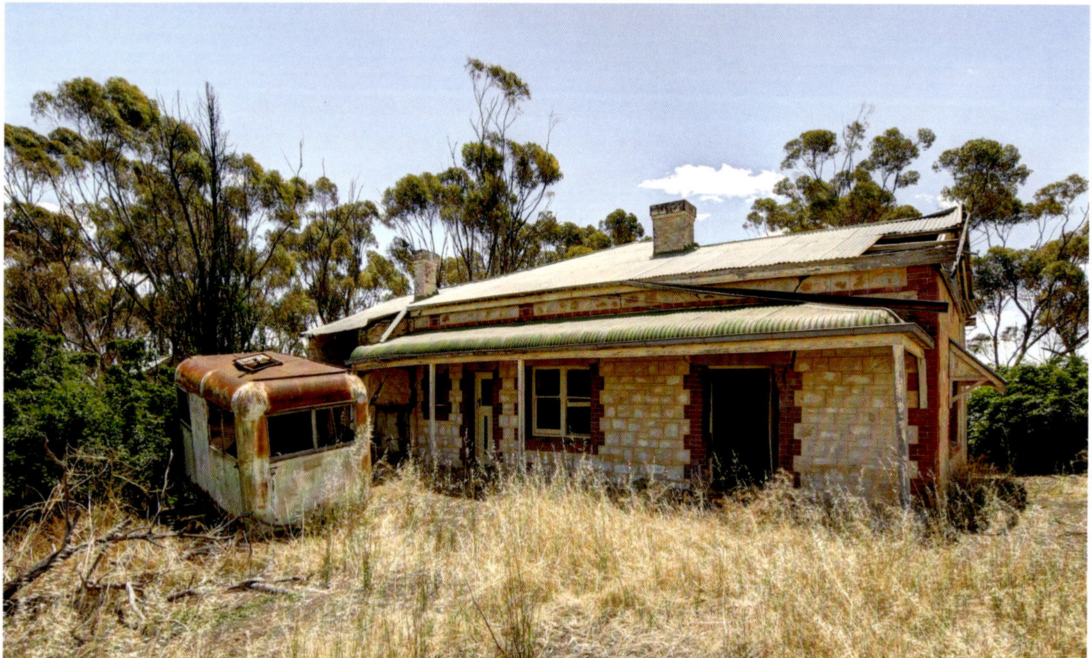

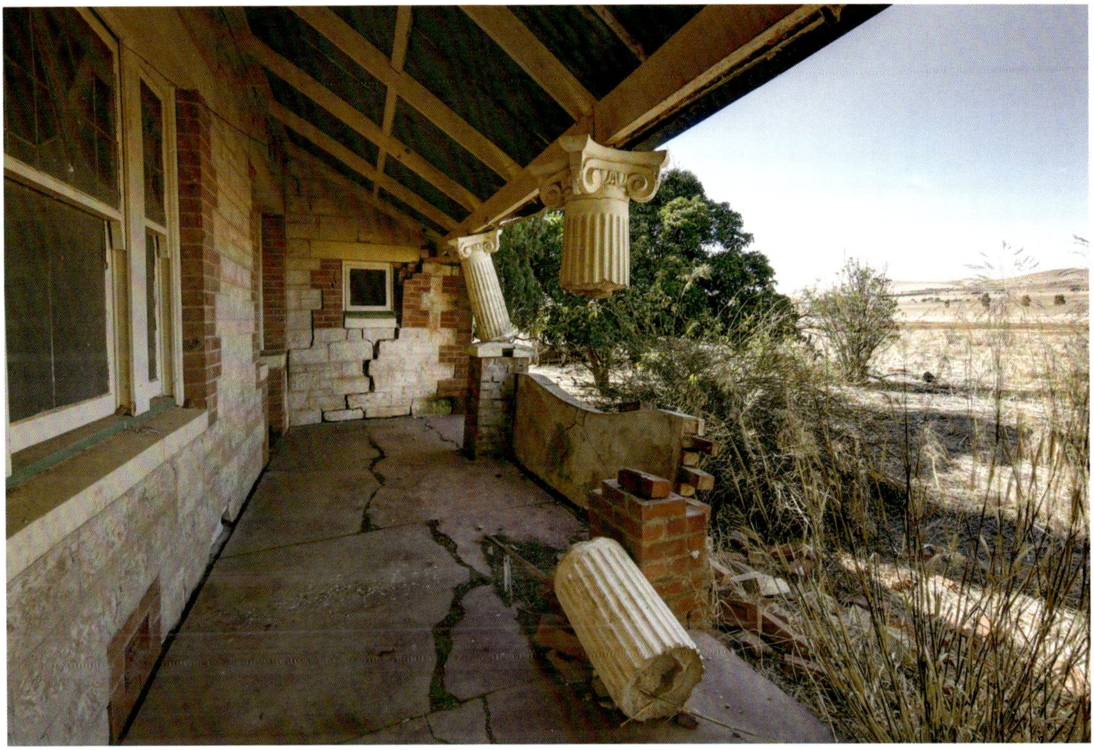

Time has collapsed the front porch of a discarded home.

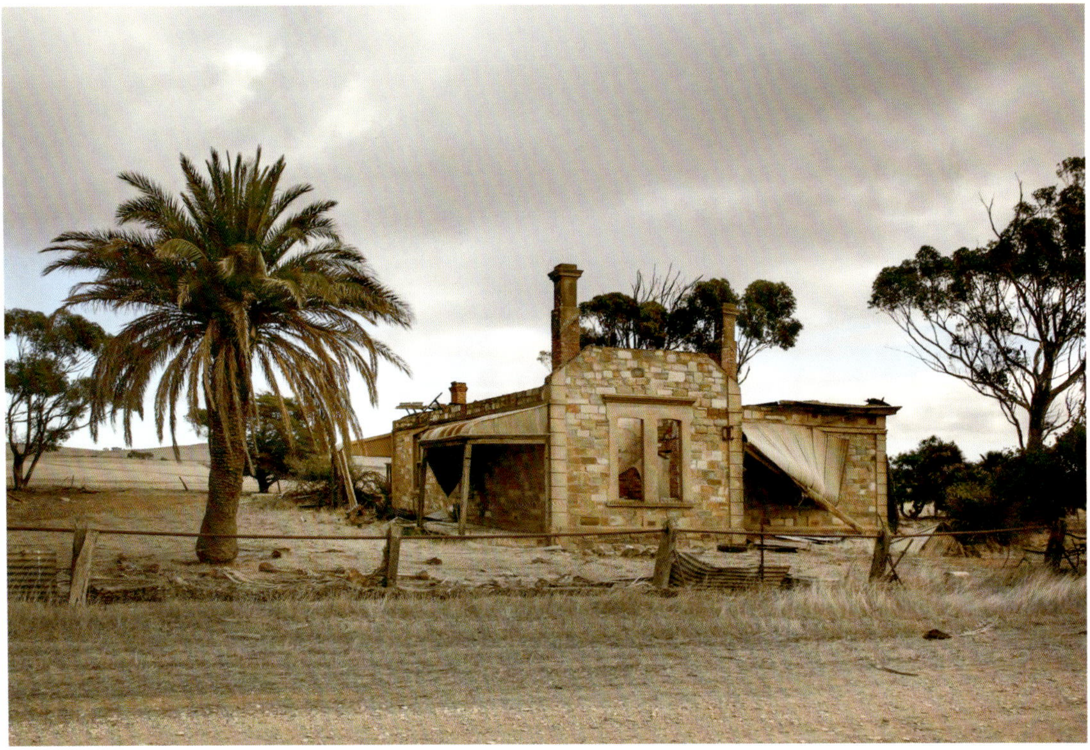

The shell of a once prominent homestead.

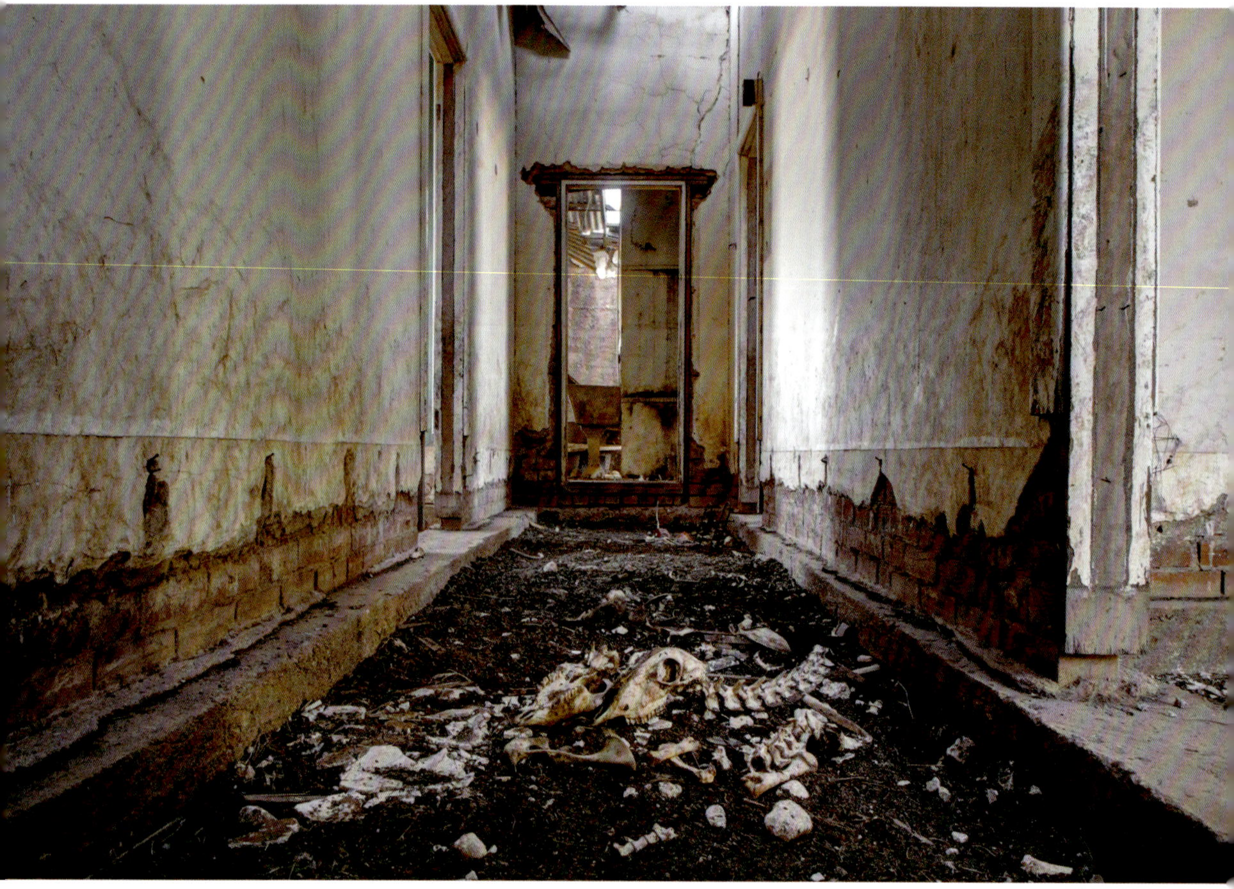

The interiors of derelict farmhouses are often the final resting places for sheep and cattle.

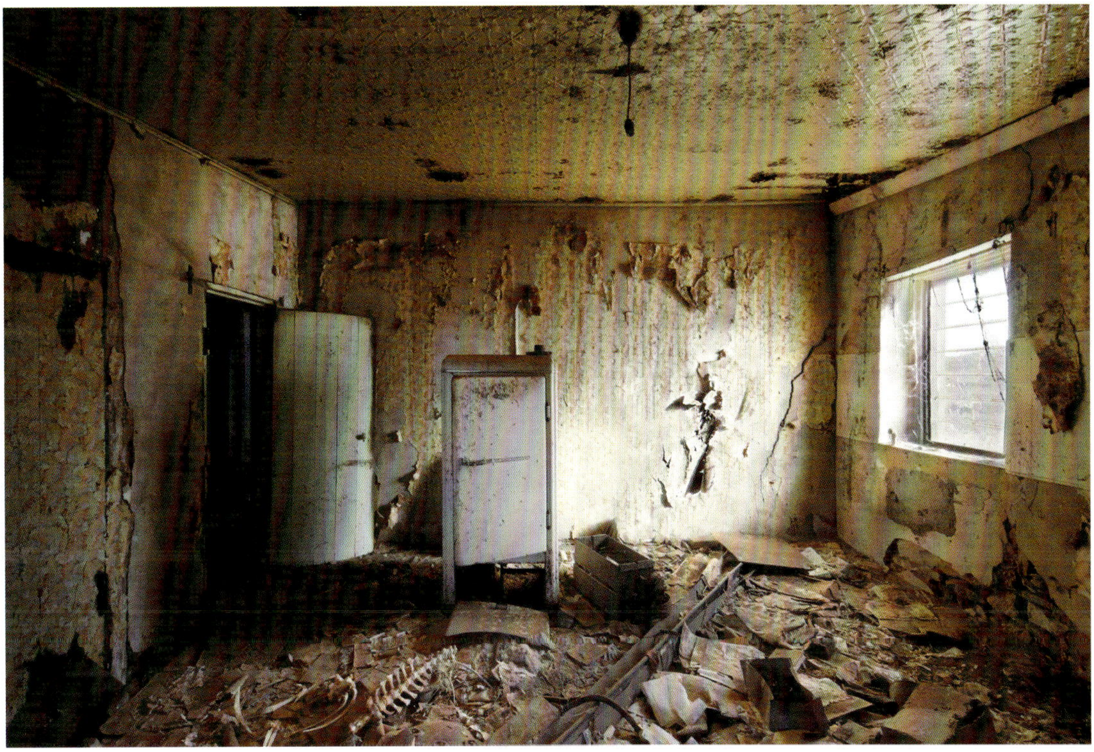

The debris and bone-filled interior of a former kitchen.

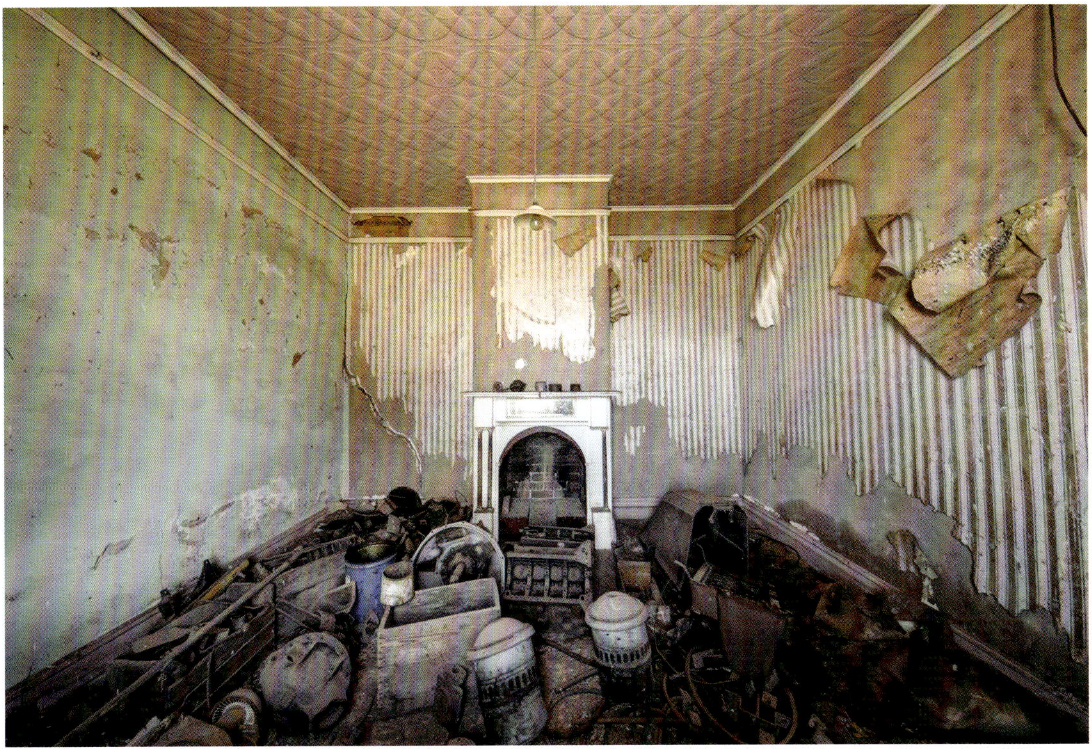

Farmers sometimes utilise the rooms of old homesteads as storage spaces. Over the years, discarded farming artefacts gather dust and melt back into the earth.

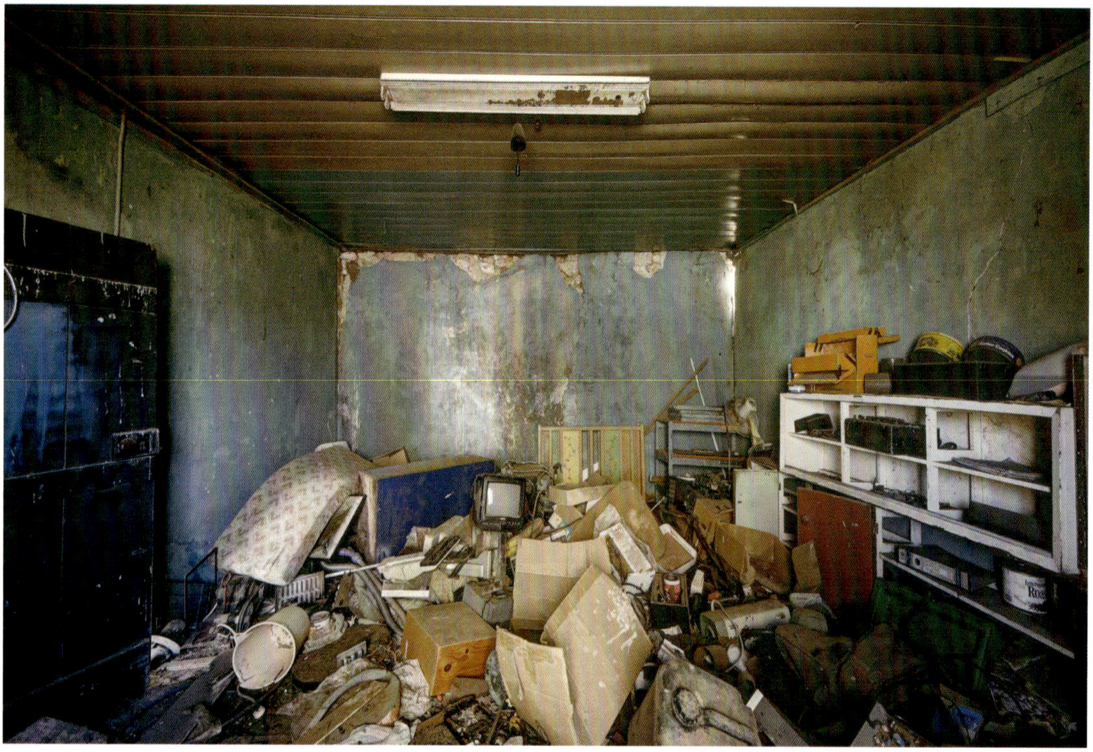

The clutter of years long past litters the floor of a room in this now derelict cottage.

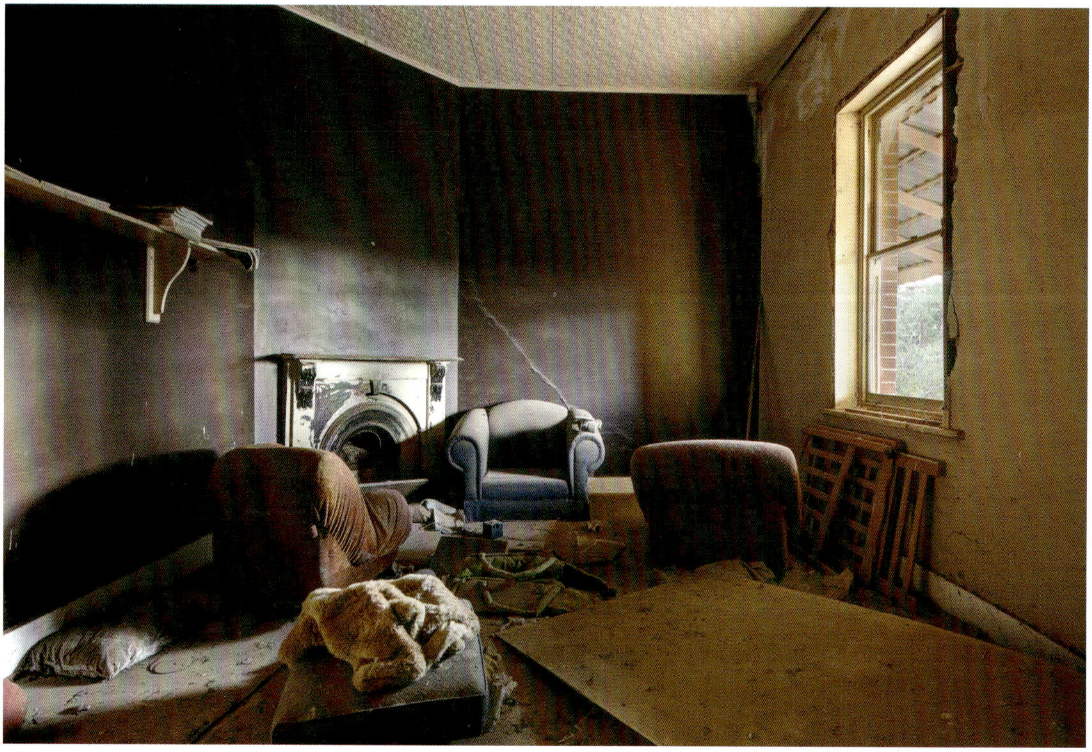

A forgotten lounge room with an original fireplace and mantle.

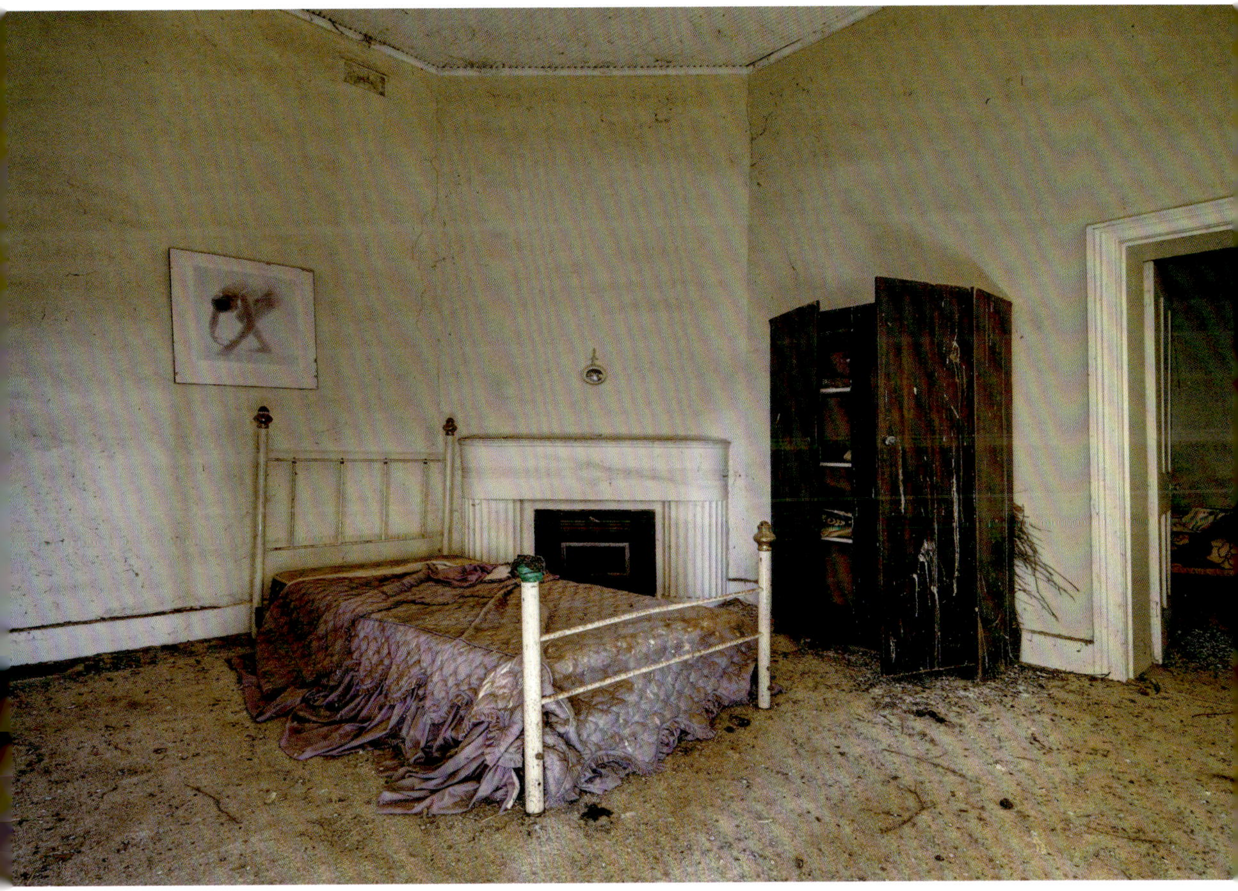

The bedroom of a still fully furnished farmhouse left to decay. Art Deco mantelpieces are a common feature in most war-period homes.

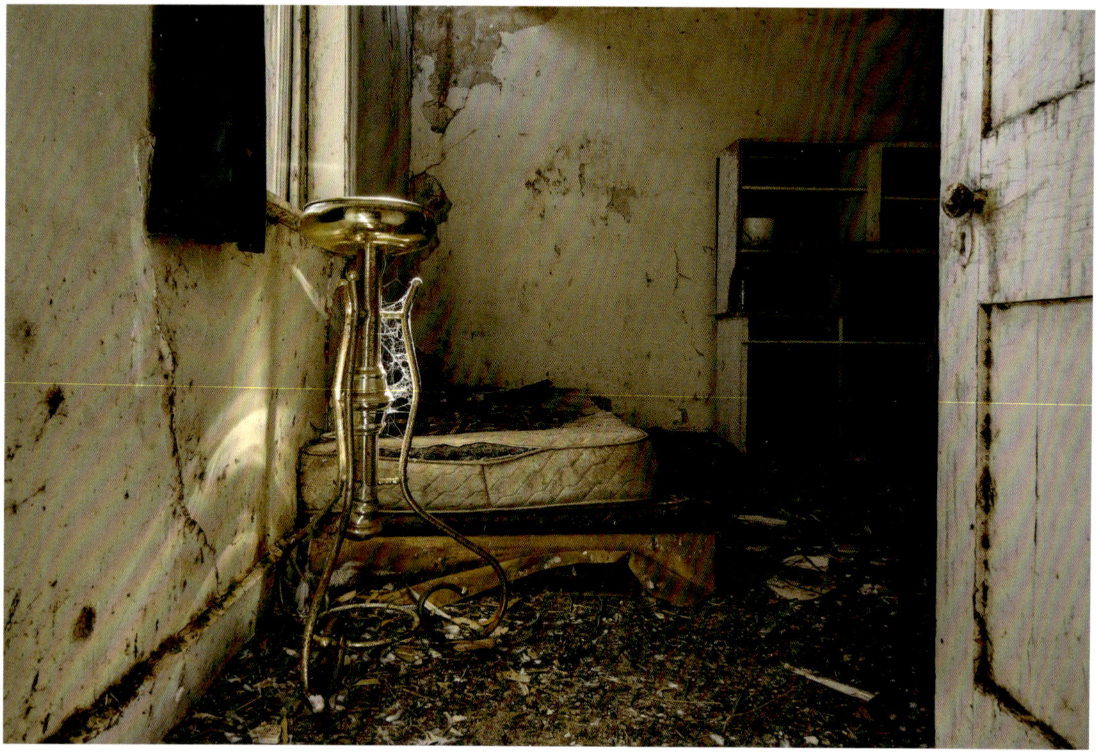

The stale scent of cigarette smoke still lingers in the rooms of many abandoned houses.

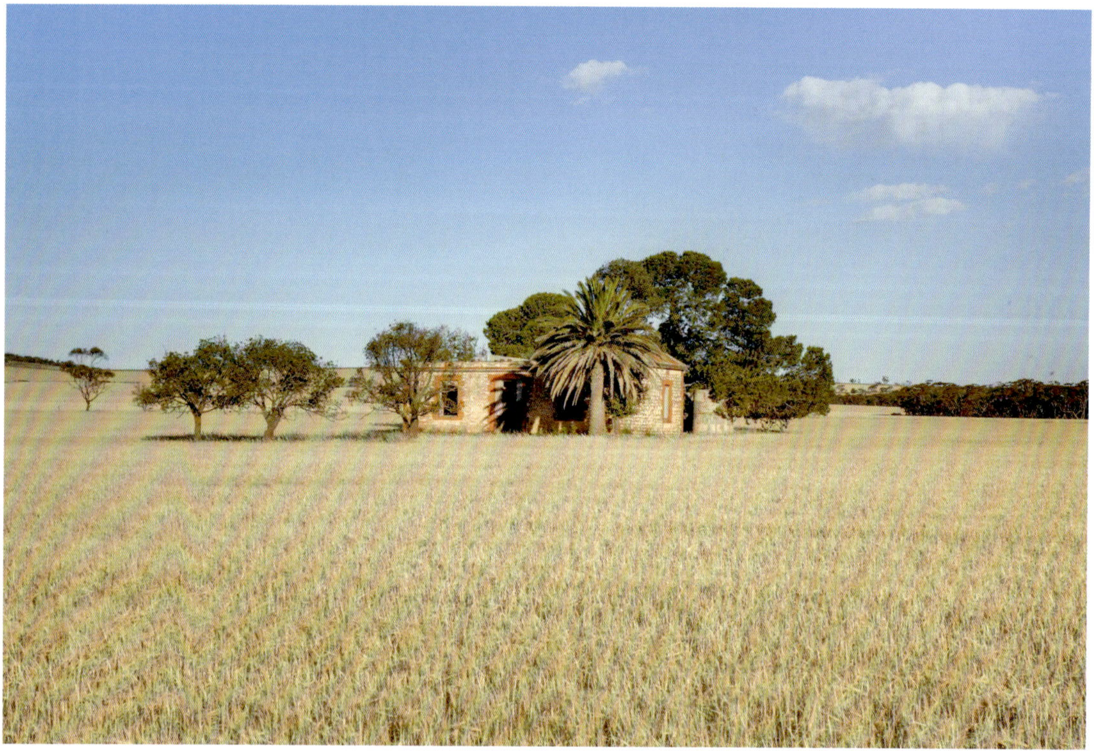

A dilapidated farmhouse near Worlds End.

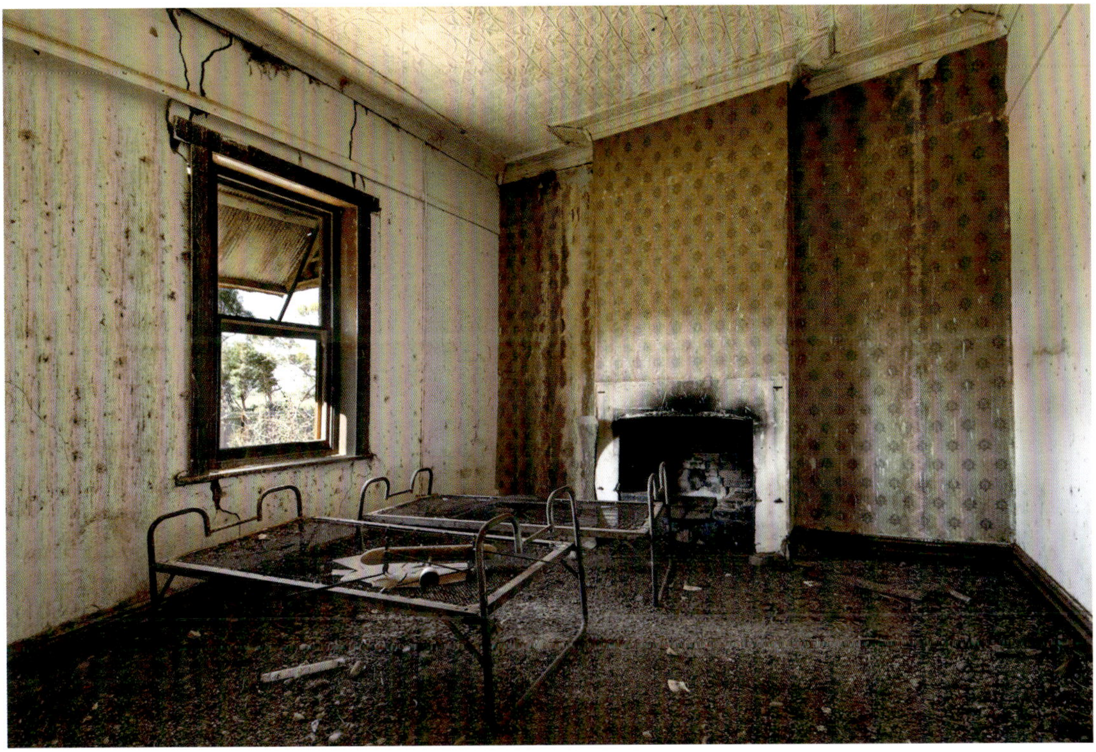

Two rusted bedframes attempt to stitch together the now dissolved stories of rural family life.

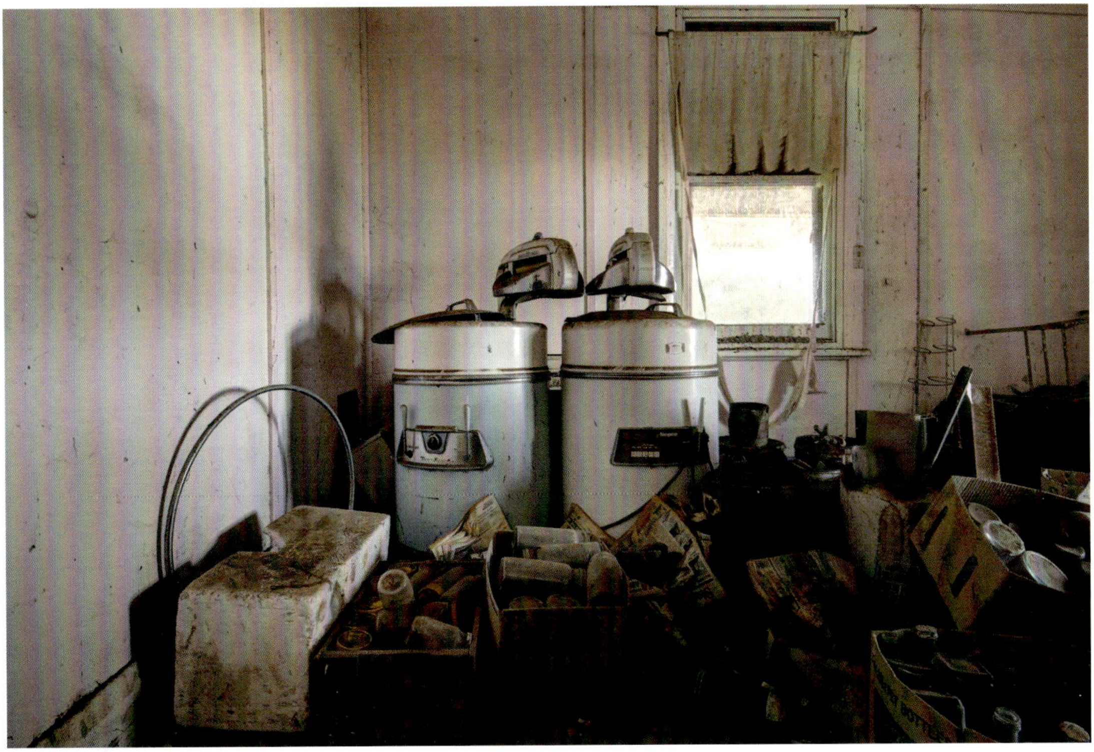

Dust now replaces what were once grimy farmer's clothes in these vintage Simpson washing machines.

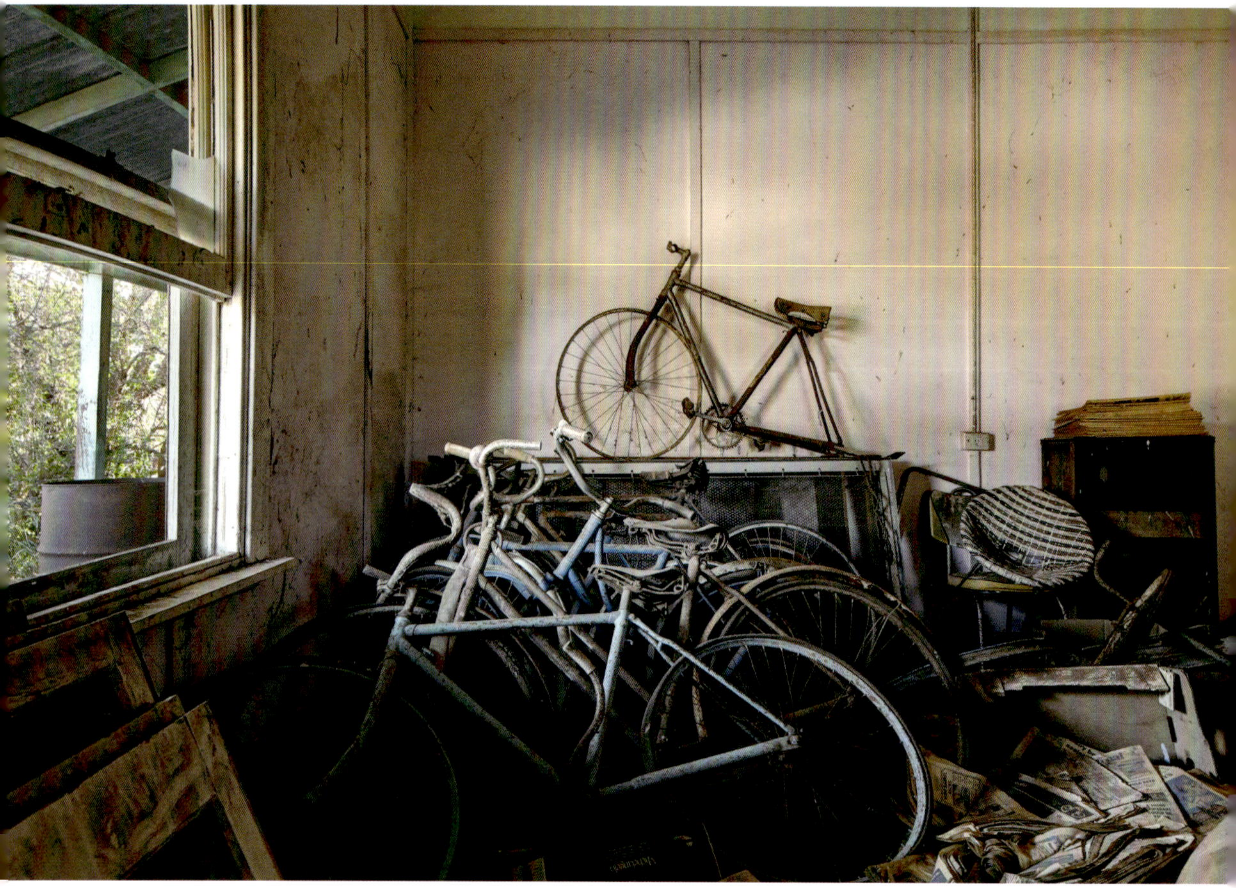

A collection of old bicycles gathers cobwebs in the lounge of a weathered farmhouse.

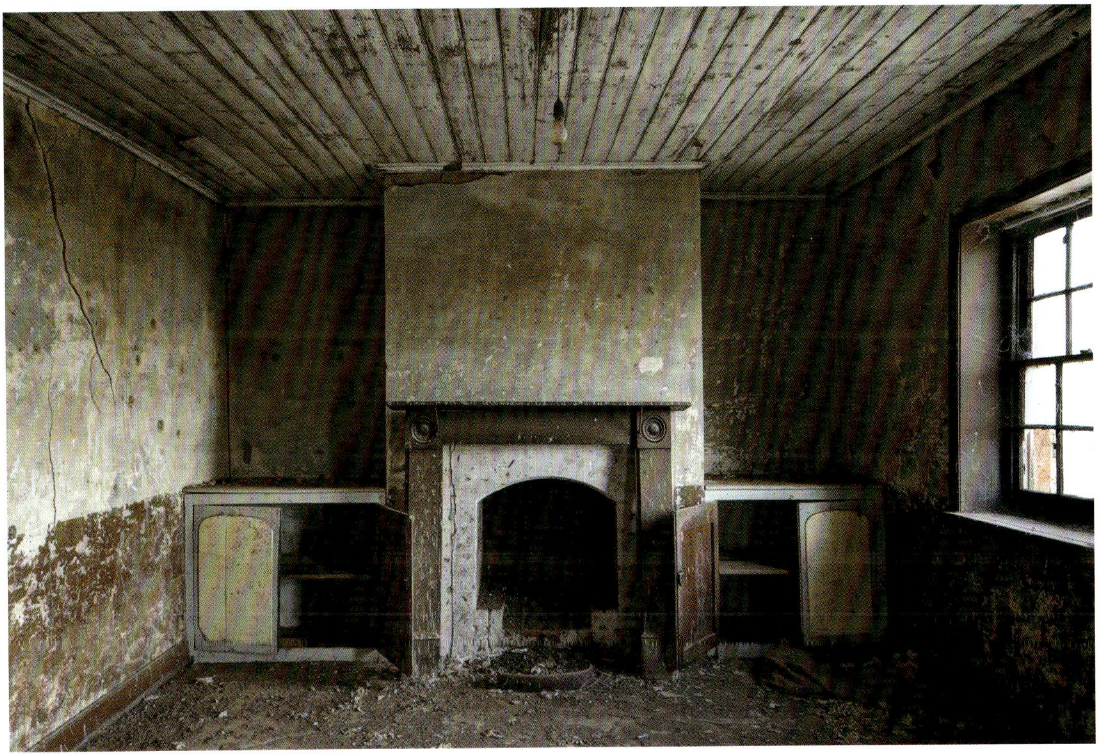

A lounge interior with its original fireplace and wooden mantle.

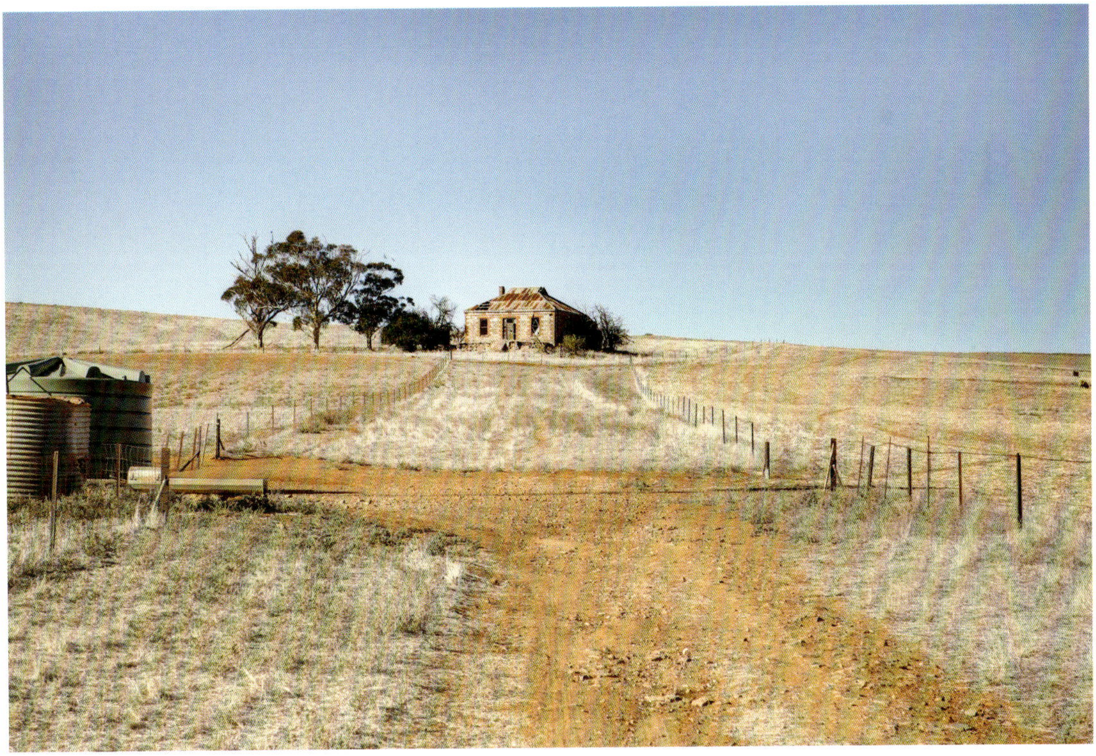

A farmhouse baking in the sun of the mid-north farming region of South Australia.

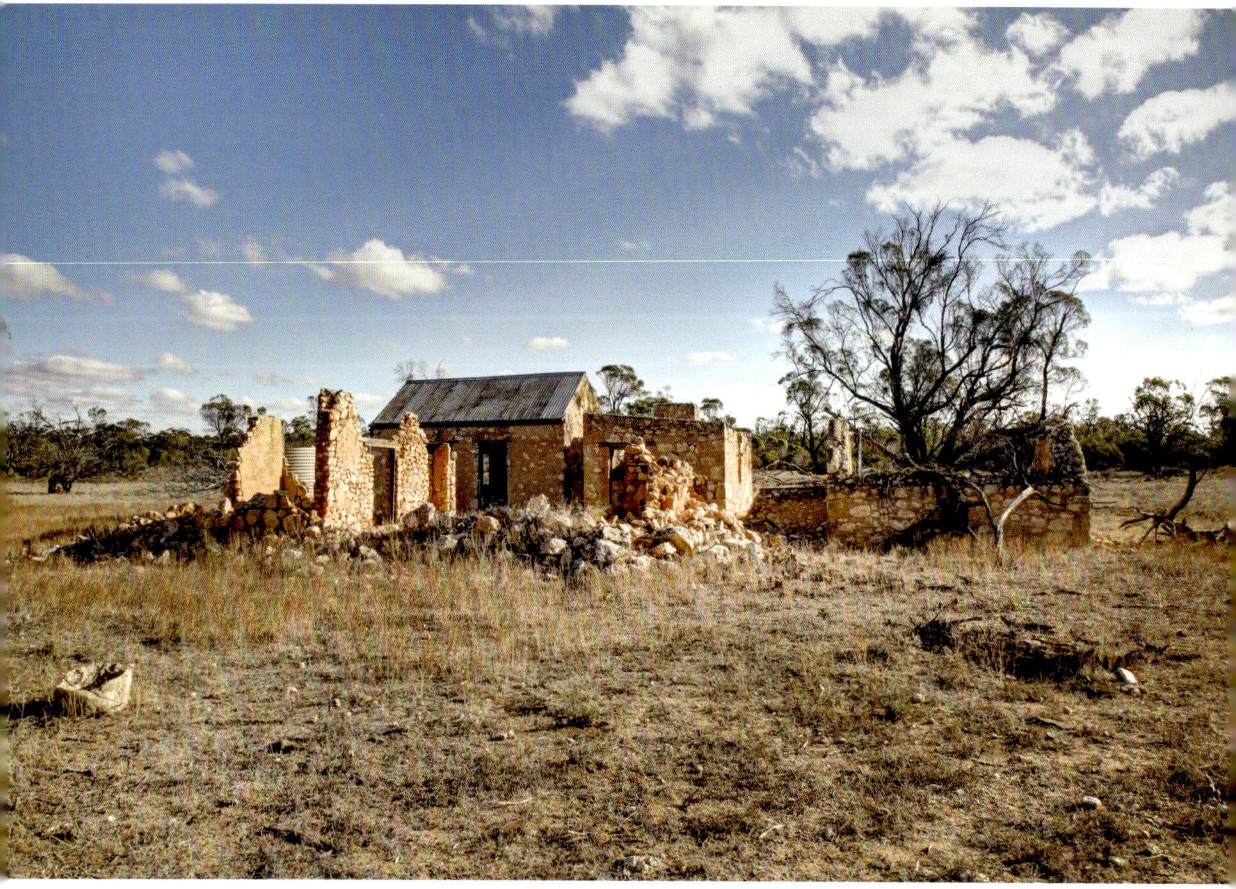

The crumbling stone ruins of a former home in the arid Murray and Mallee region.

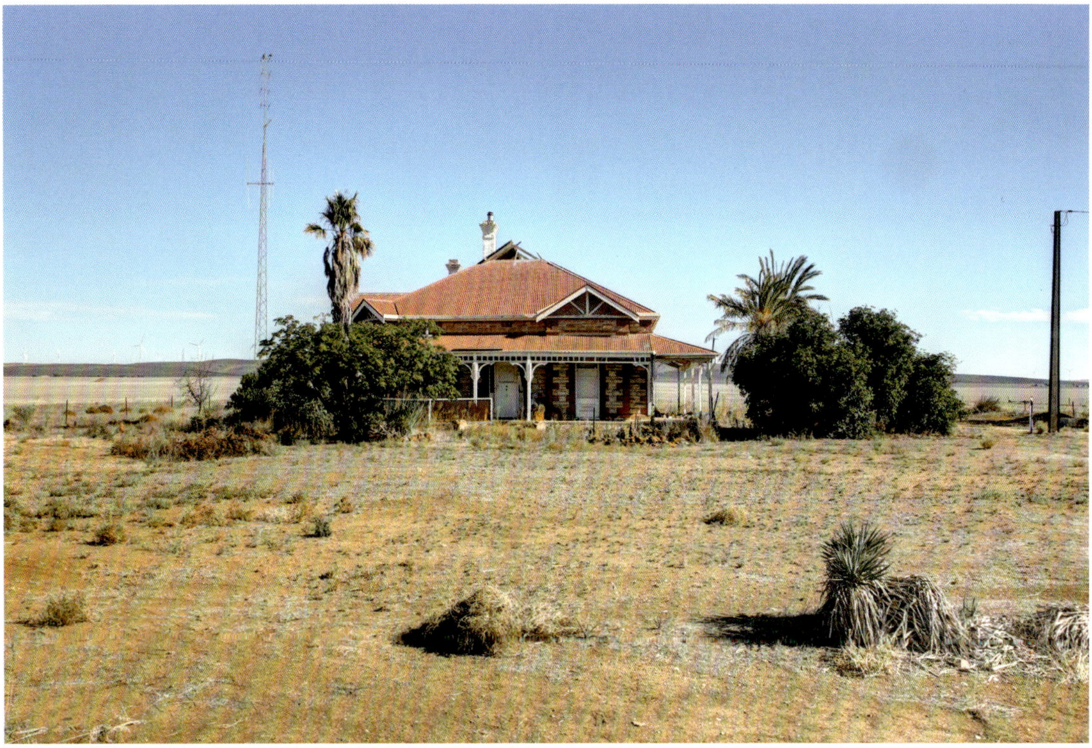

An abandoned home slowly fading away alongside a highway in South Australia's mid-north.

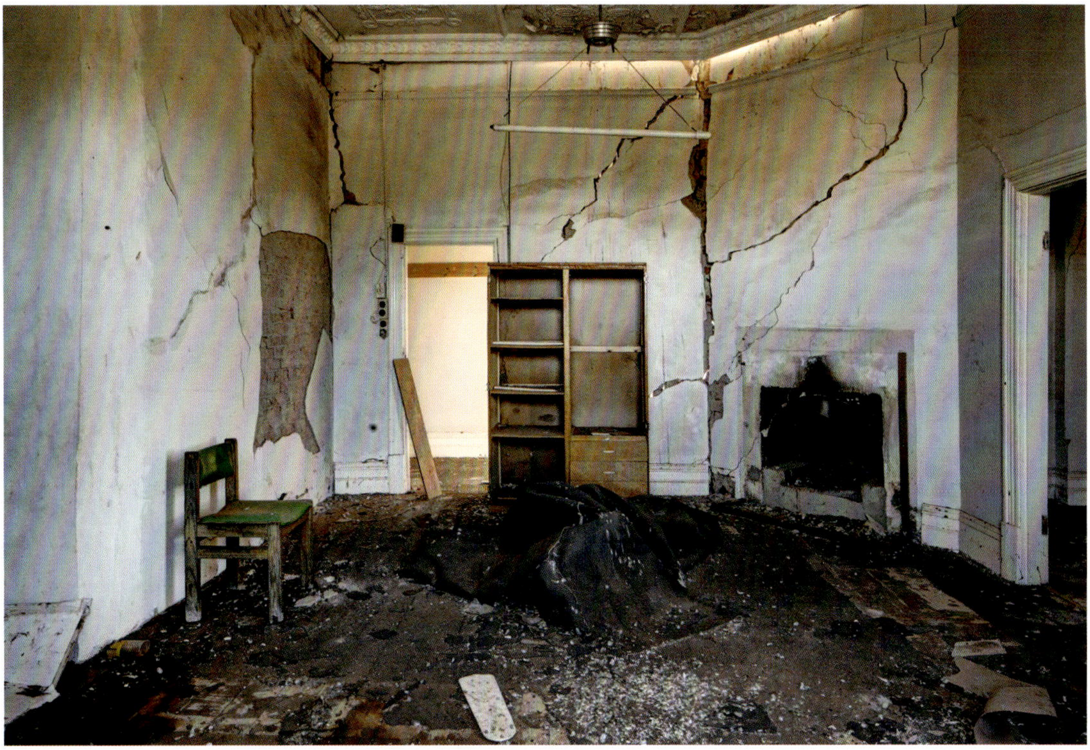

Years of no maintenance have resulted in cracked walls and peeling plaster. Seldom restored, the original cornices and patterned pressed tin ceilings in this homestead will inevitably crumble and fade away.

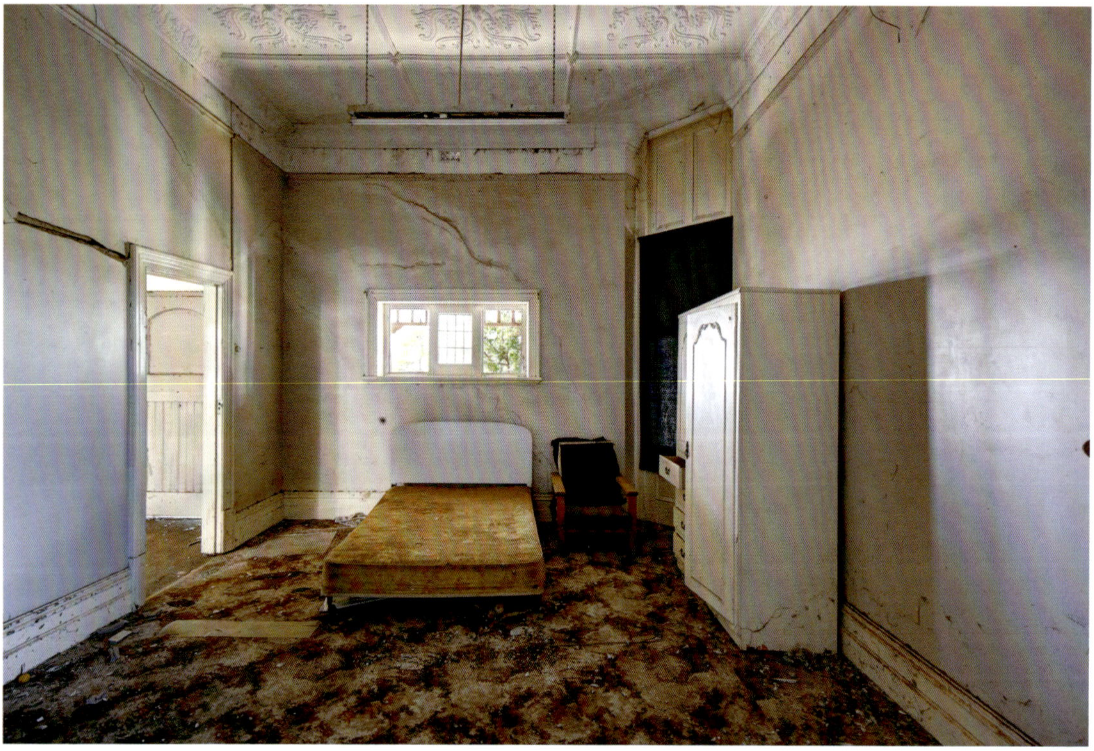

An original fluorescent light fitting clings desperately to the pressed tin ceiling of this former master bedroom.

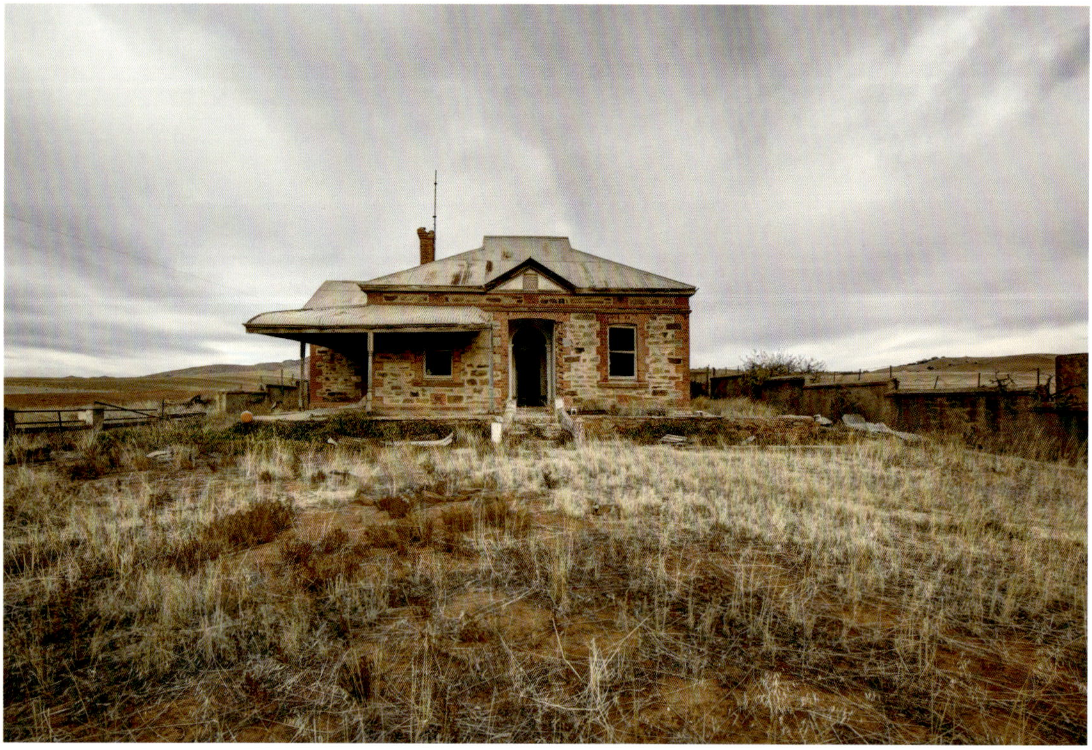

A homestead in north-eastern South Australia.

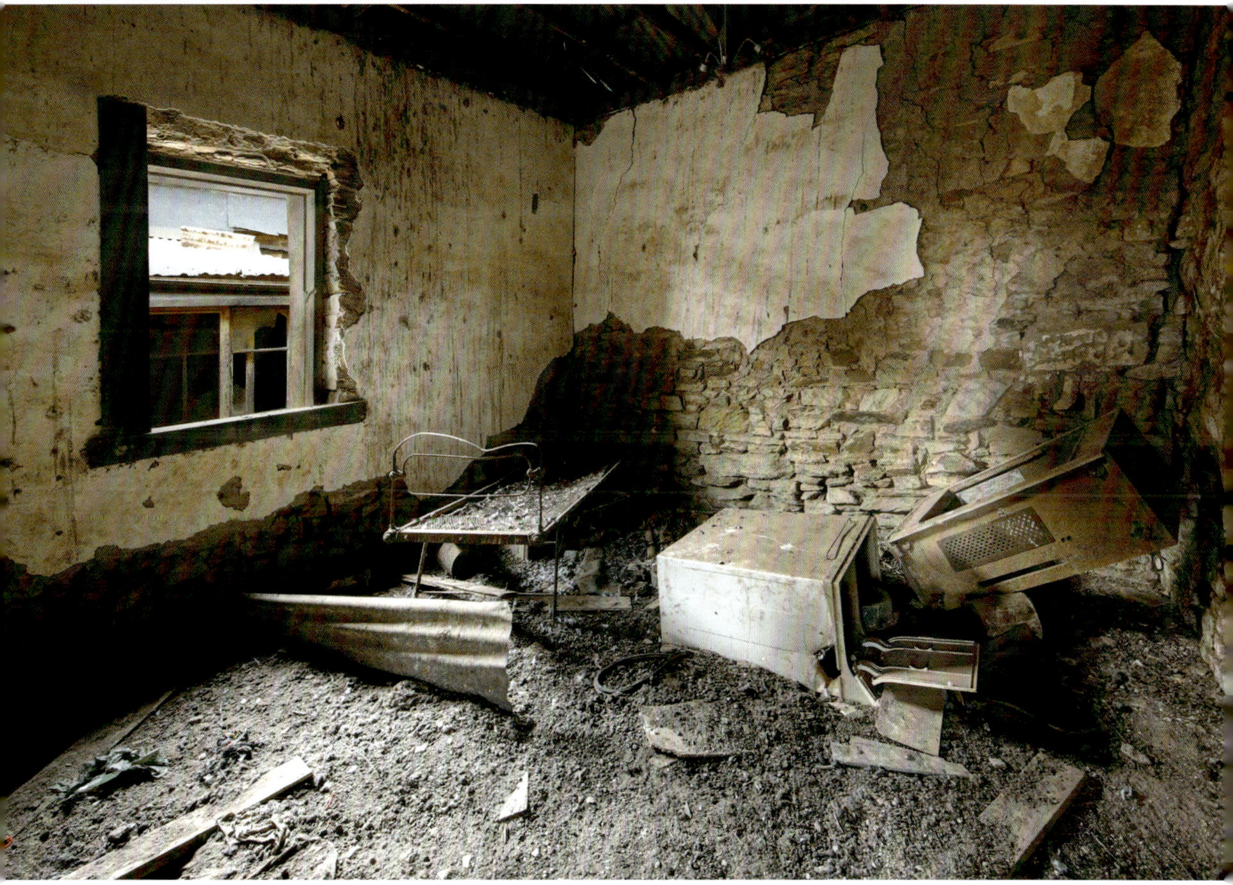

A room still contains the household artefacts from residents long since past.

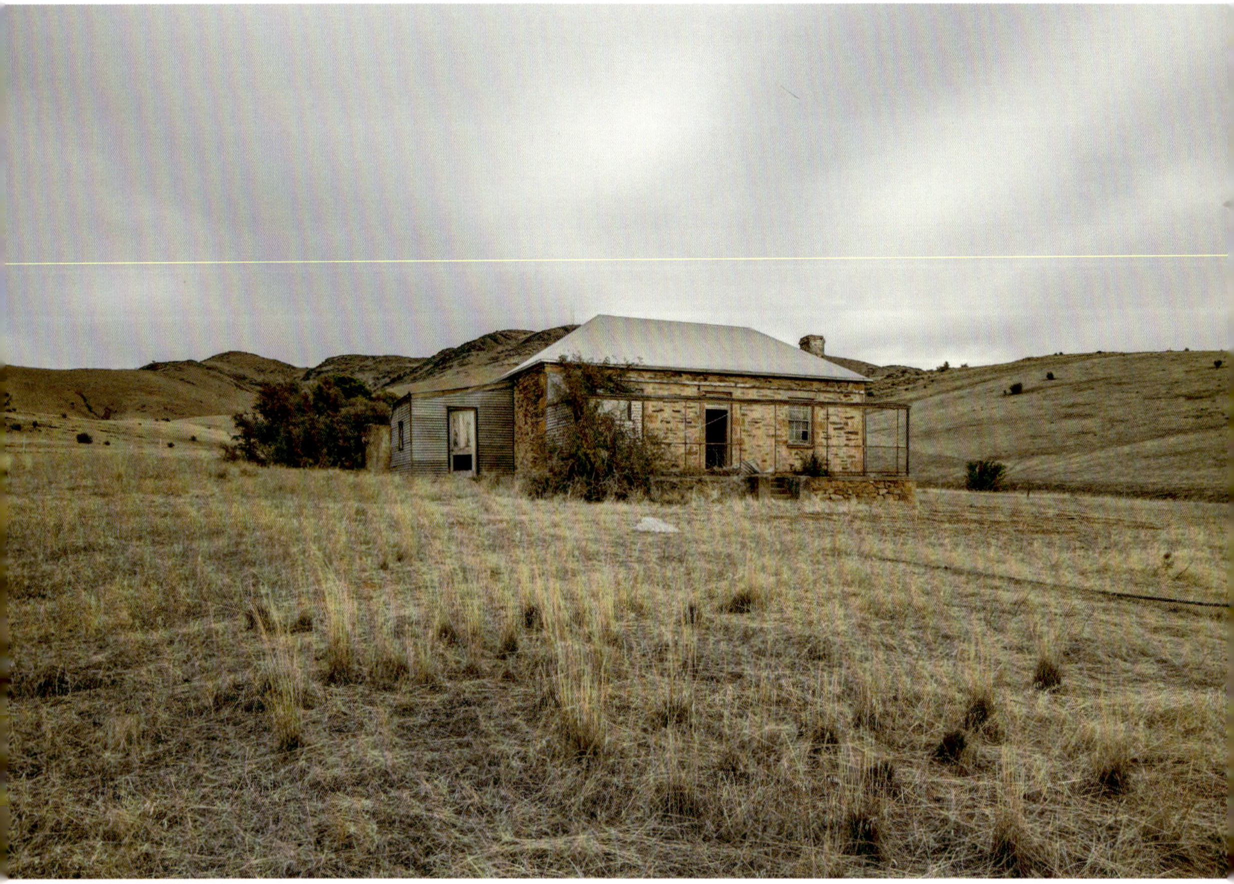

A simple yet weathered homestead sits atop a hill in the rural farming regions of the state's north-east.

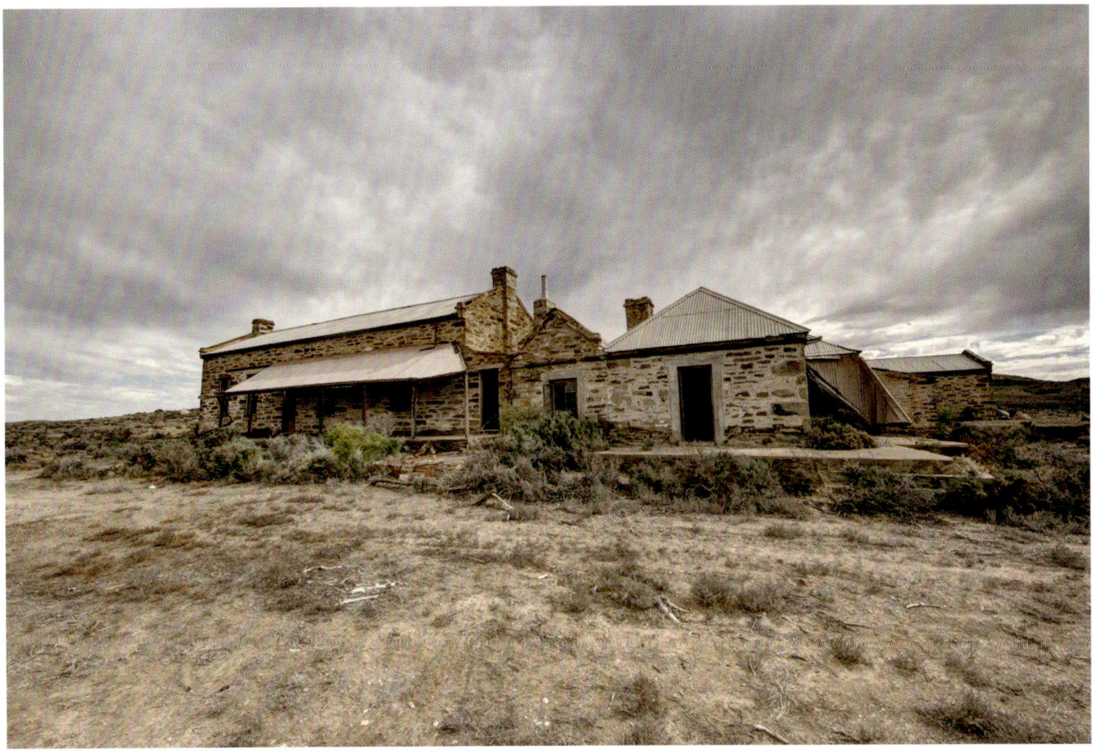

Surrounded by salt bush and open plains, this resilient stone and timber building has survived after years of dust storms and floods. A former sheep station, the establishment once housed a succession of tired herders.

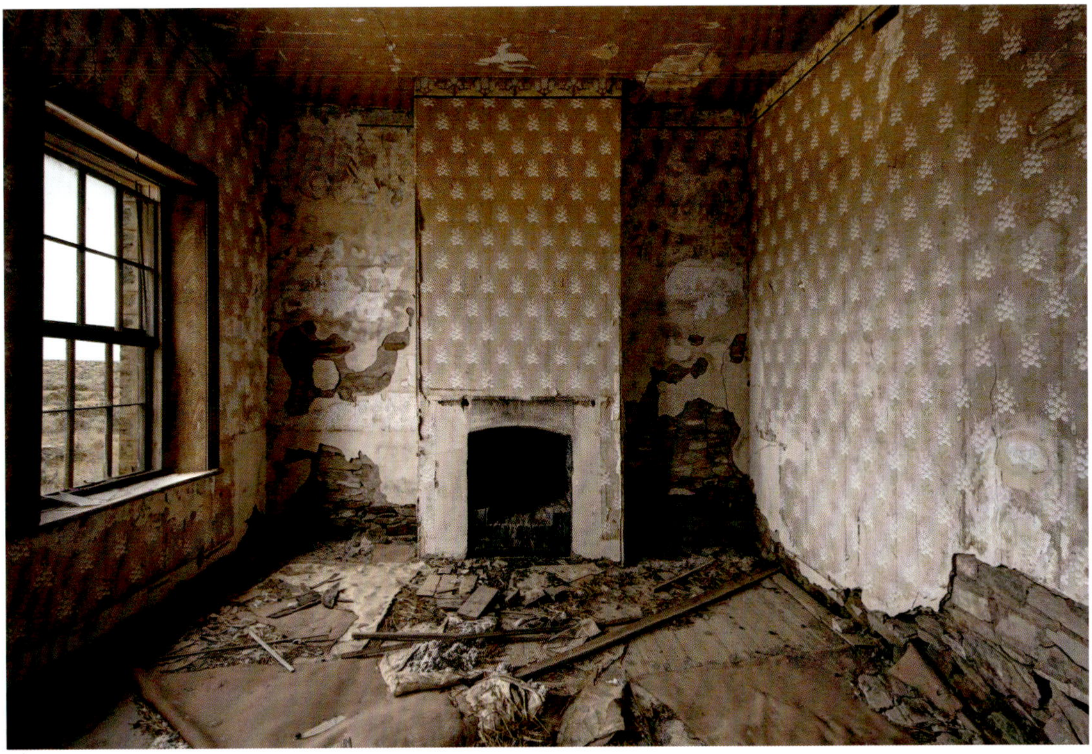

This sheep station's interior still contains original patterned cornices.

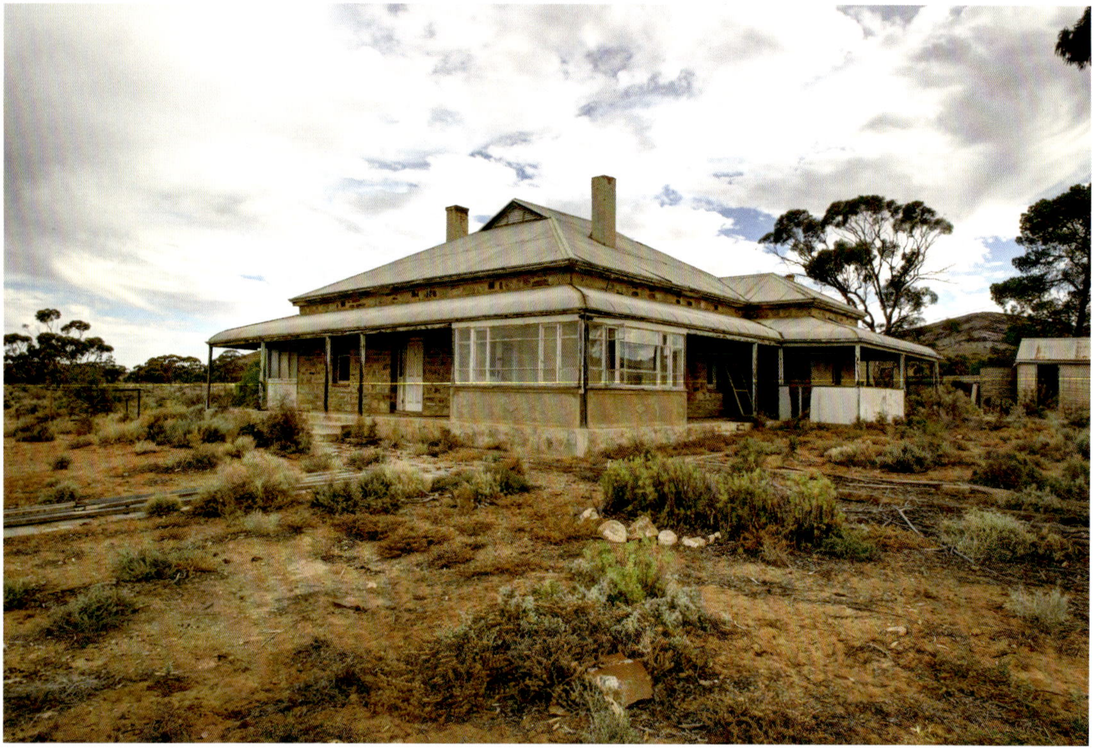

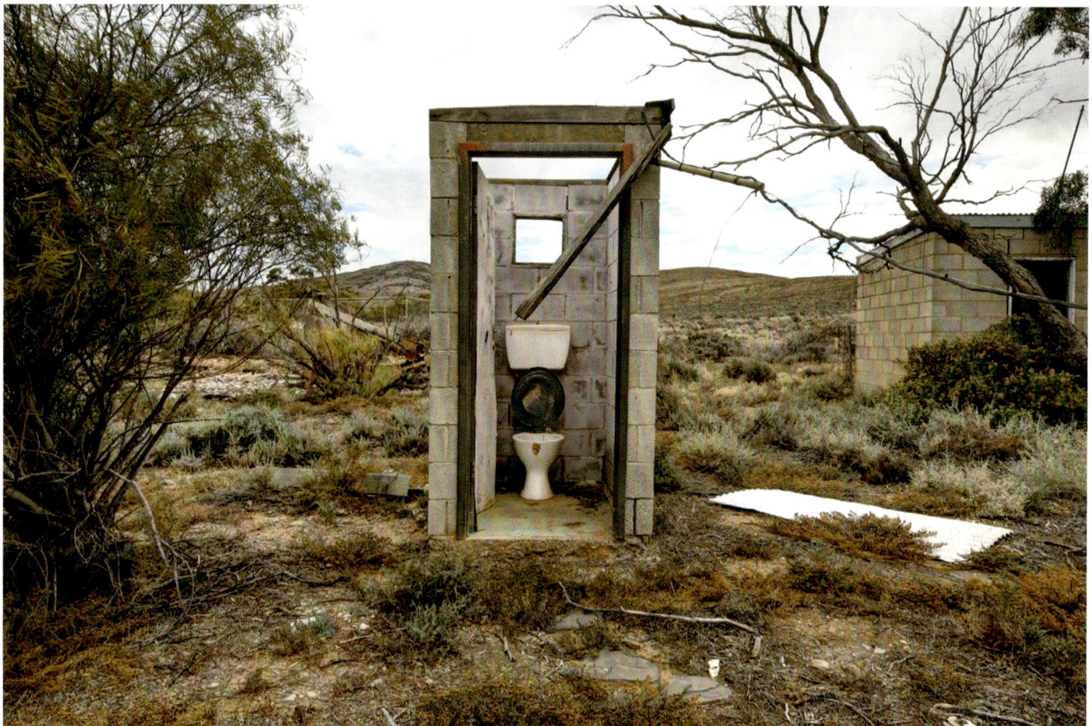

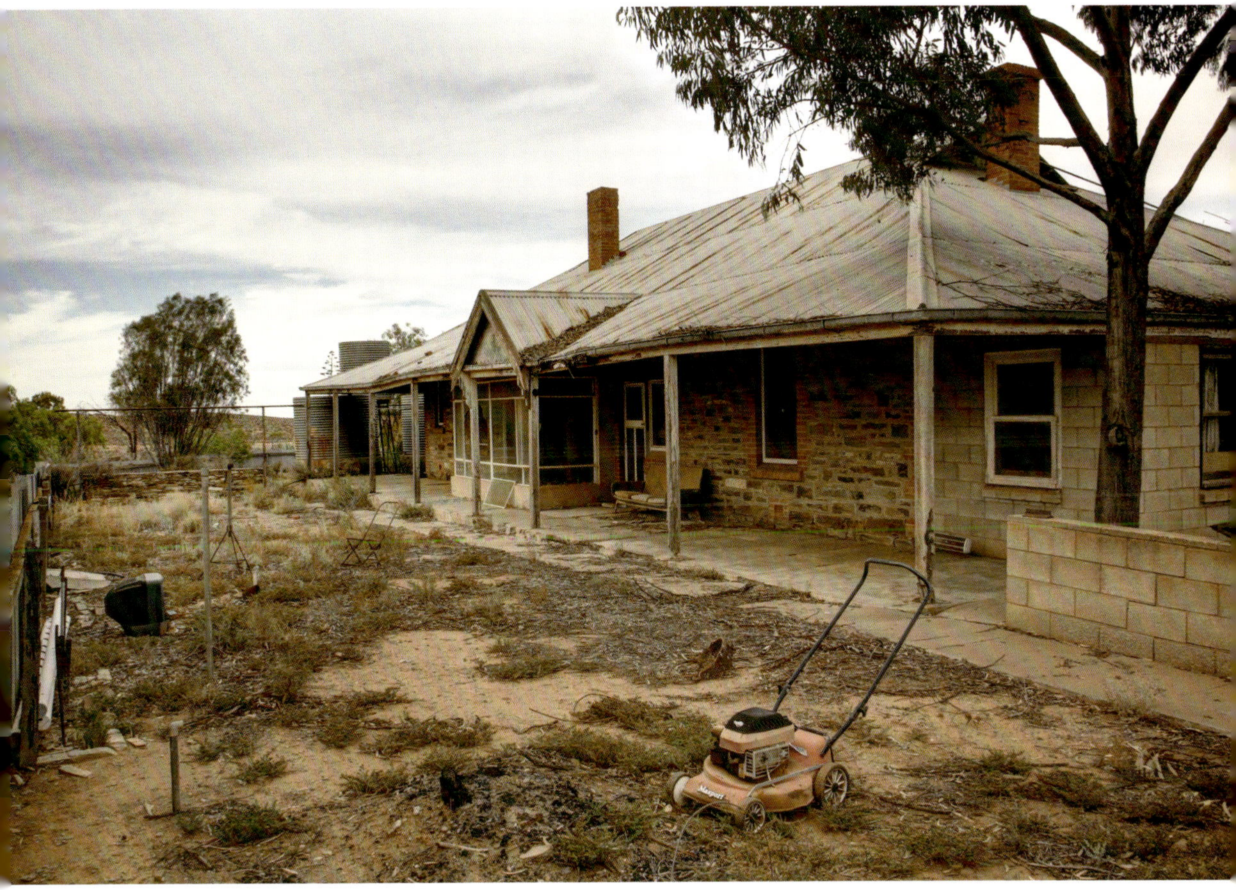

The front yard of this abandoned mid-northern homestead speaks of domestic days long since past.

Opposite above: This discarded structure was once a charming well-lit homestead. Backdropped by open rolling country, hints of its original interior can be found behind its peeling wallpaper.

Opposite below: The infamous 'outdoor dunny' is perhaps one of wider Australia's most recognised cultural icons. Sitting weather beaten behind a dilapidated farmhouse, the structure's roof most likely succumbed to one of the region's many fierce dust storms.

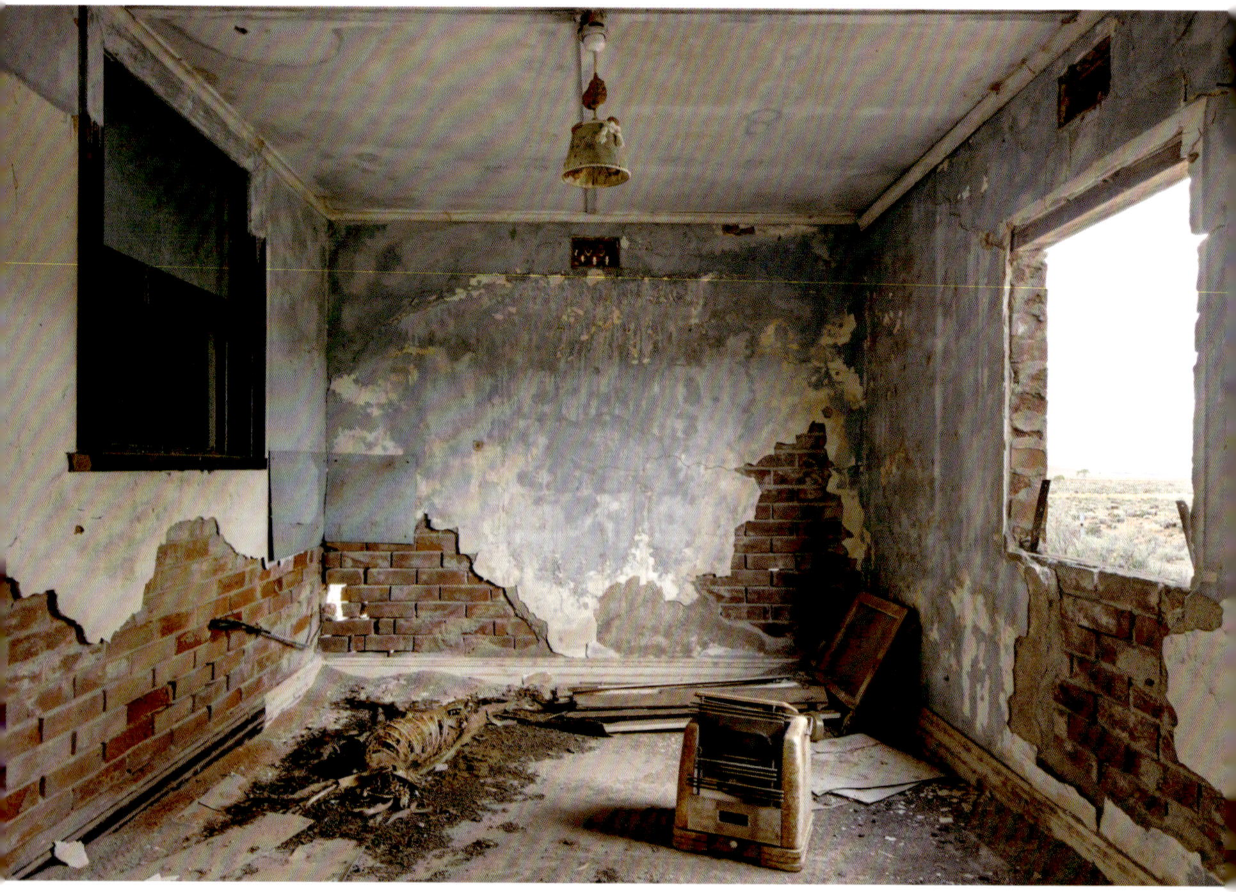

A number of desert homesteads house the rotting carcasses of hunted kangaroos.

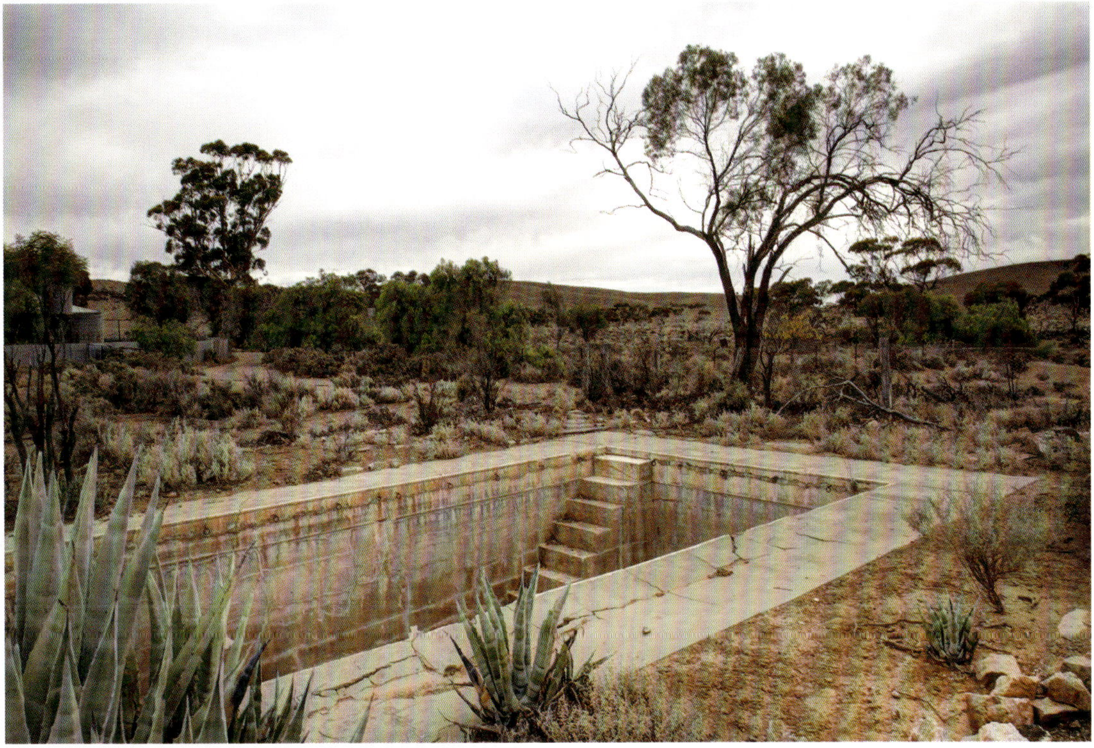

This charming former swimming pool once bathed the sweat drenched bodies of the many herders who passed through the area. Surrounded by wild succulents, the pool's steps descend into a now empty pit once filled with sparkling water that bounced the reflection of the blazing outback sun.

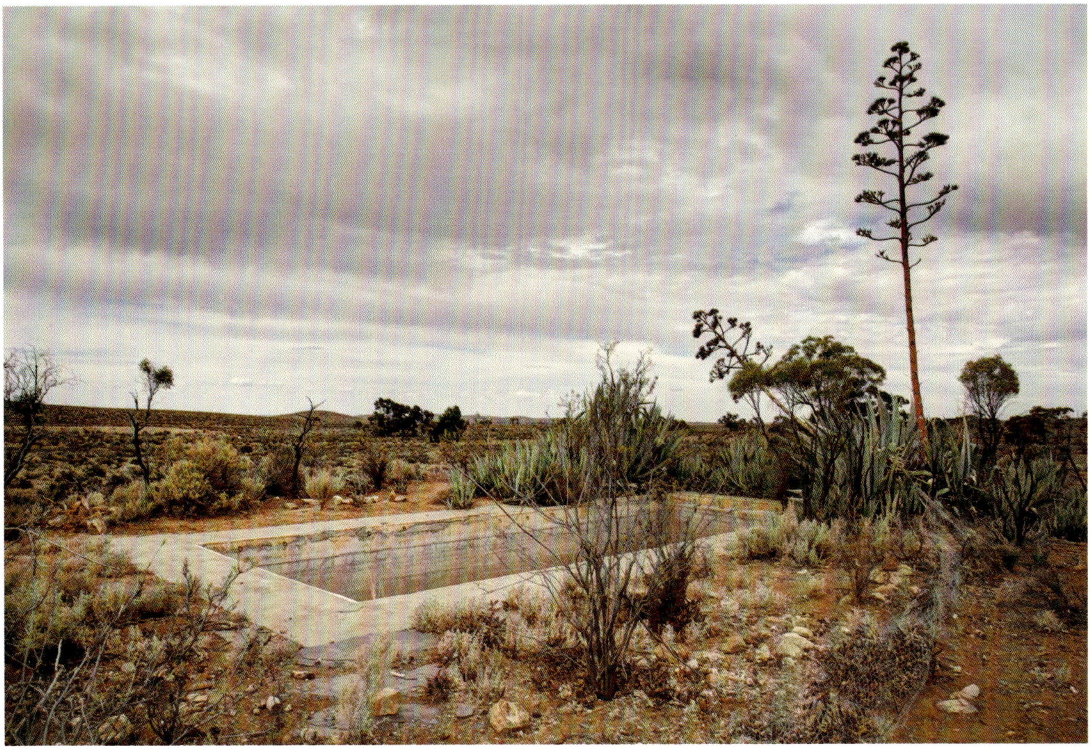

Another angle reveals the region's arid desert location.

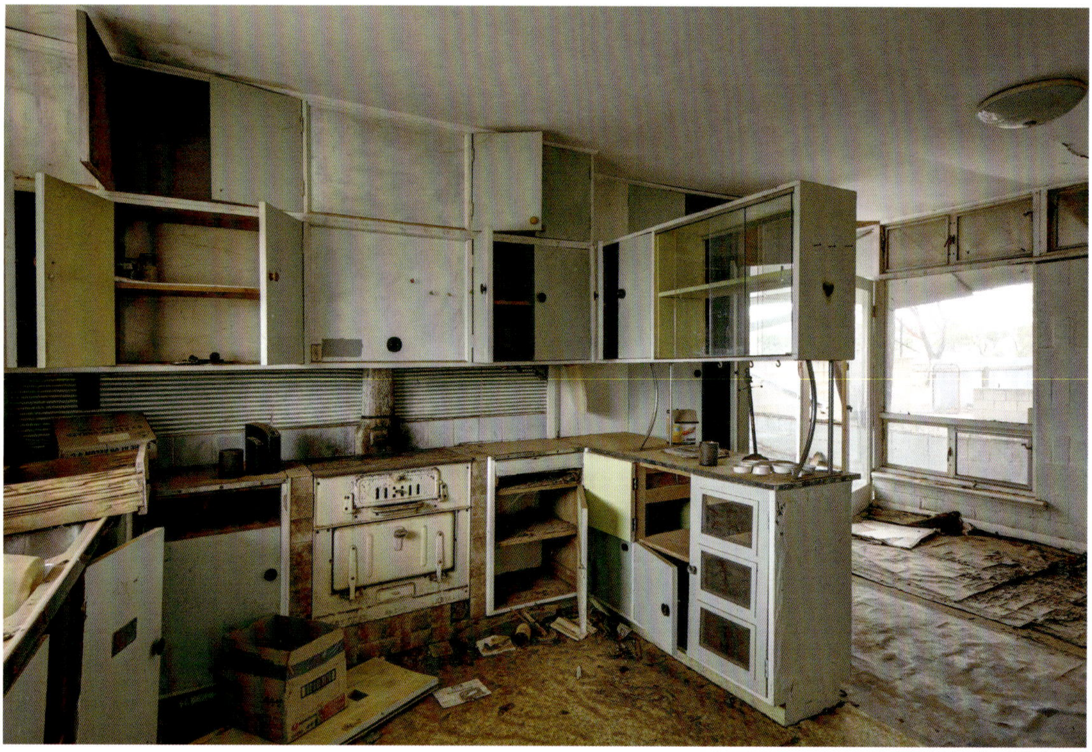

A vintage kitchen with its classic suspended overhead cabinet.

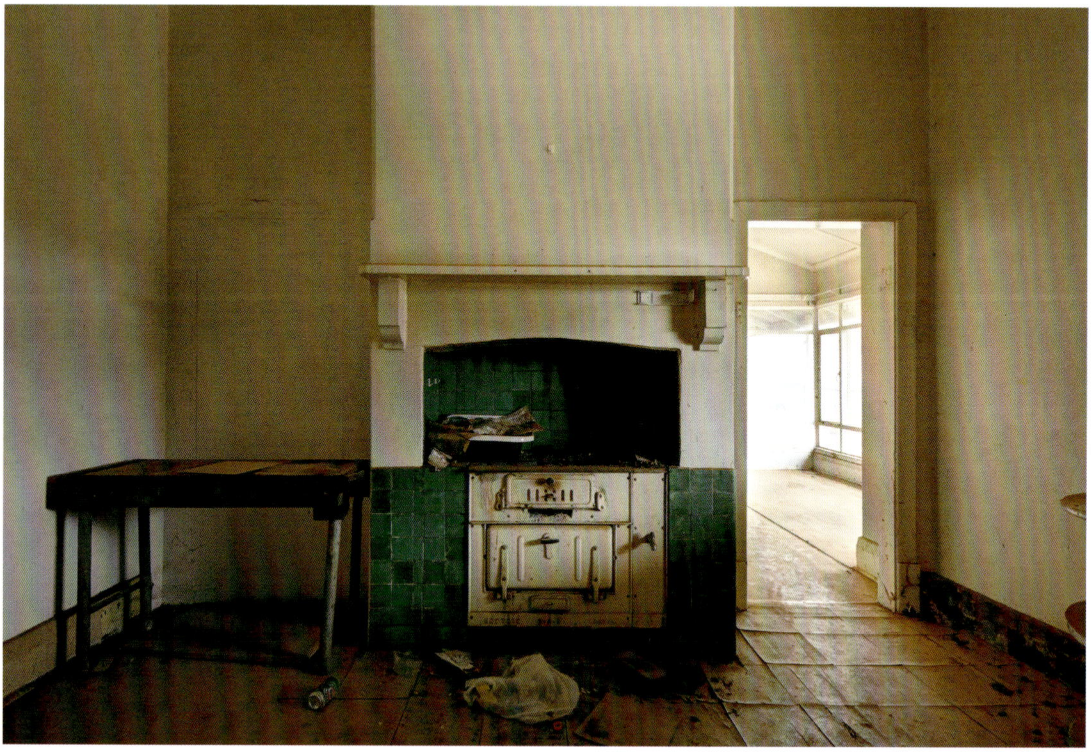

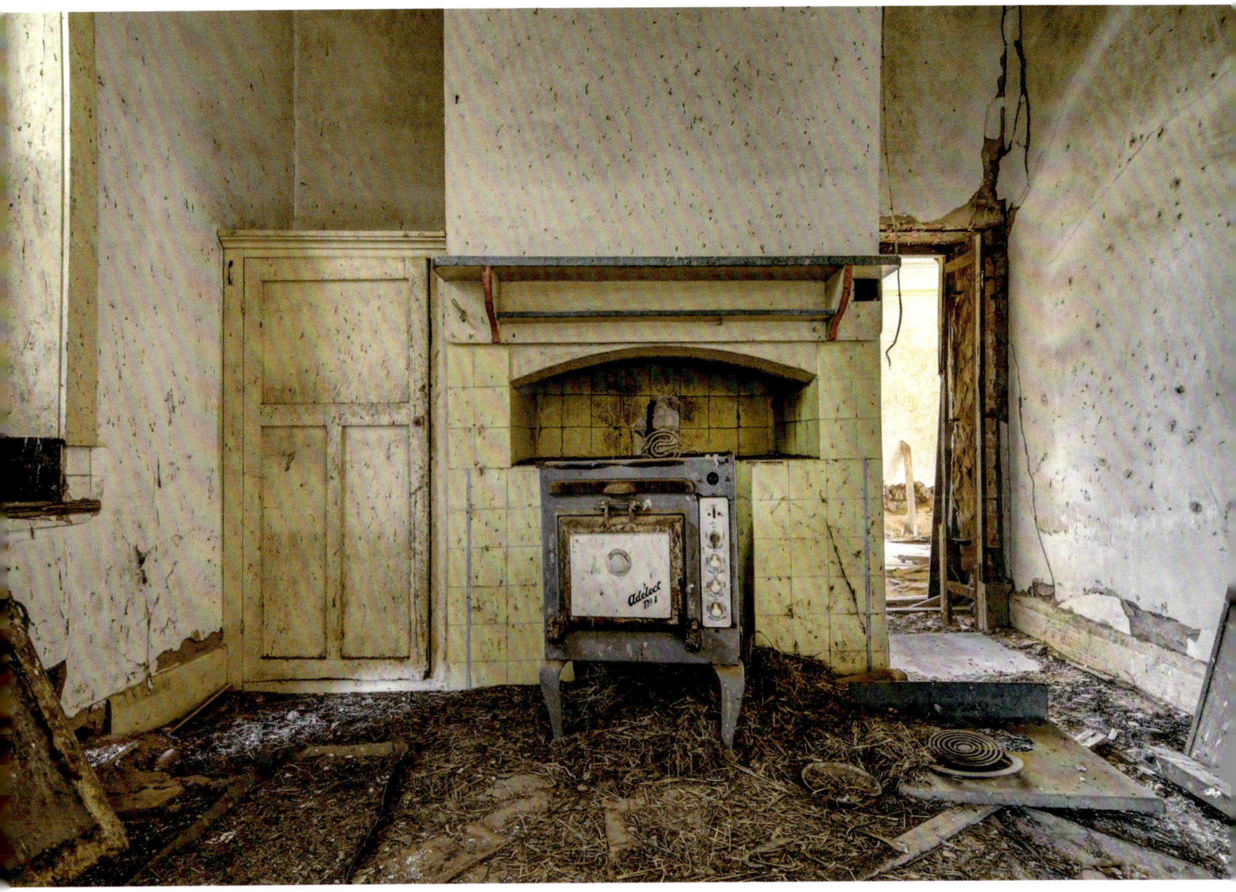

Wood-fired ovens and stoves become a regular feature inside most abandoned homesteads.

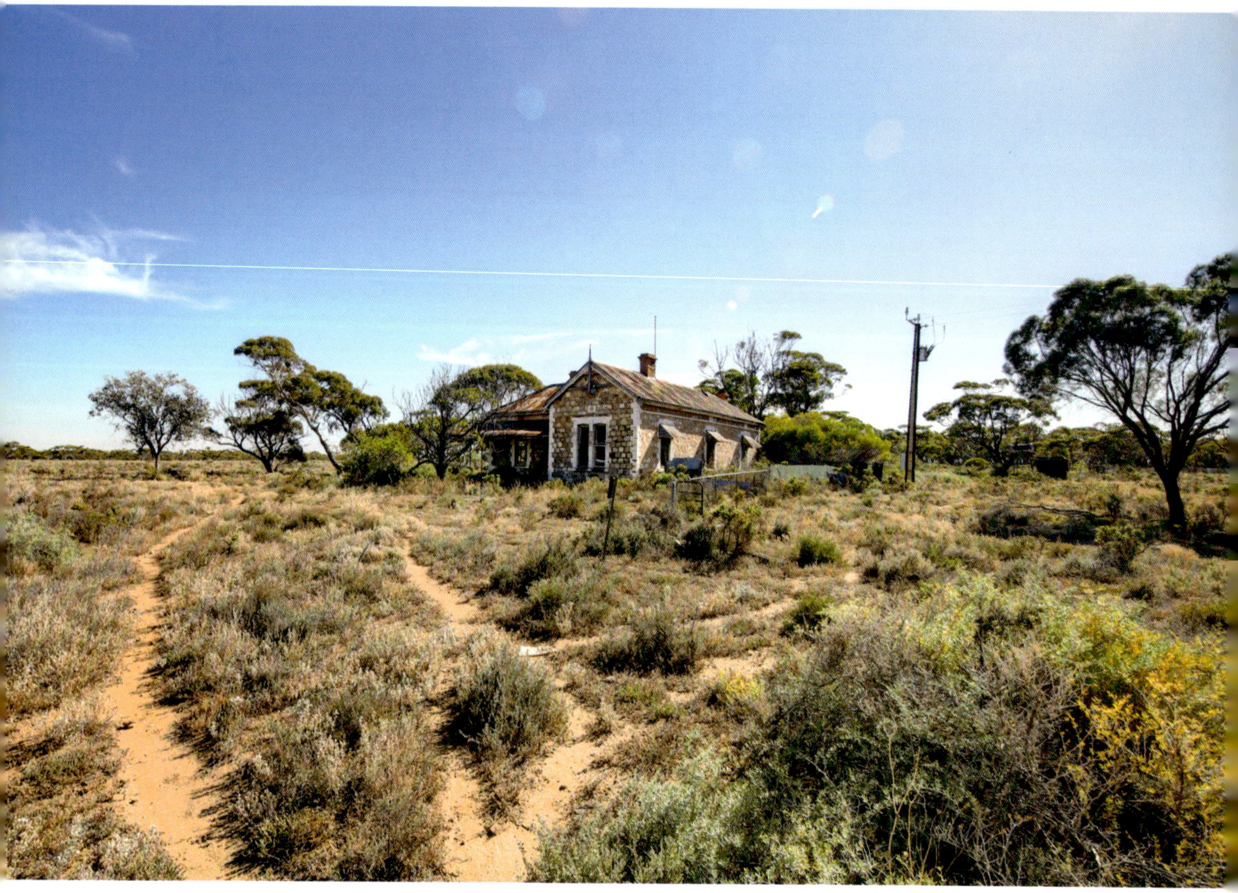

A forgotten homestead in the Spencer Gulf region.

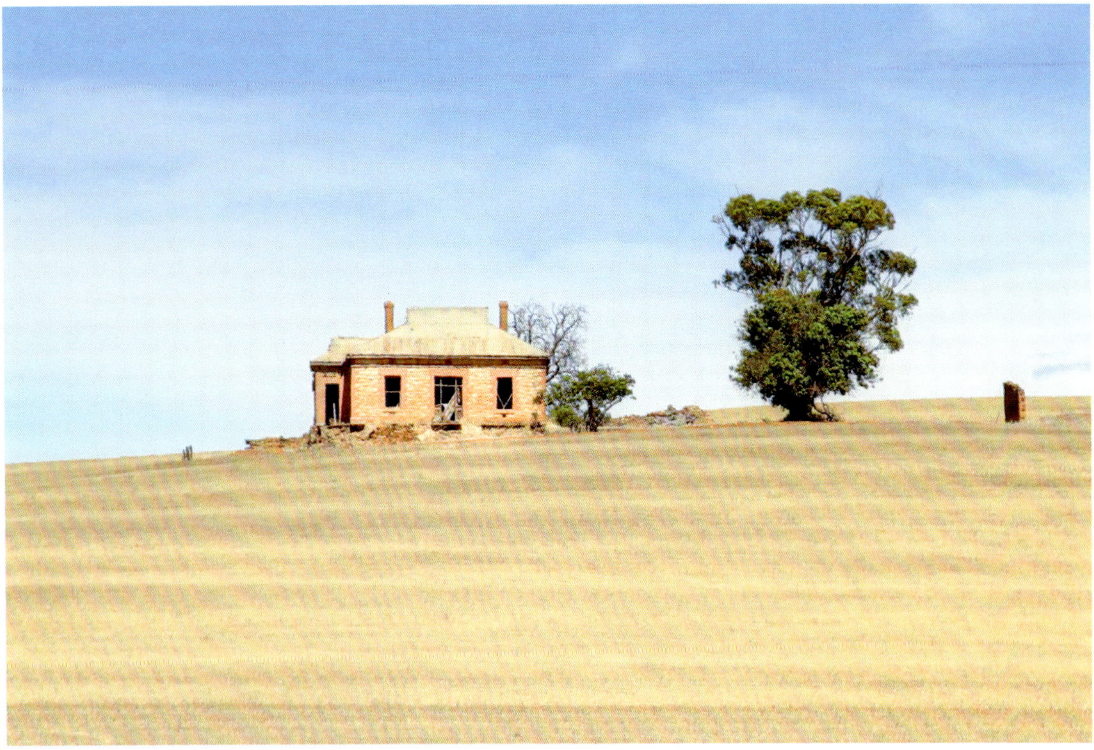

A former mid-northern farm dwelling.

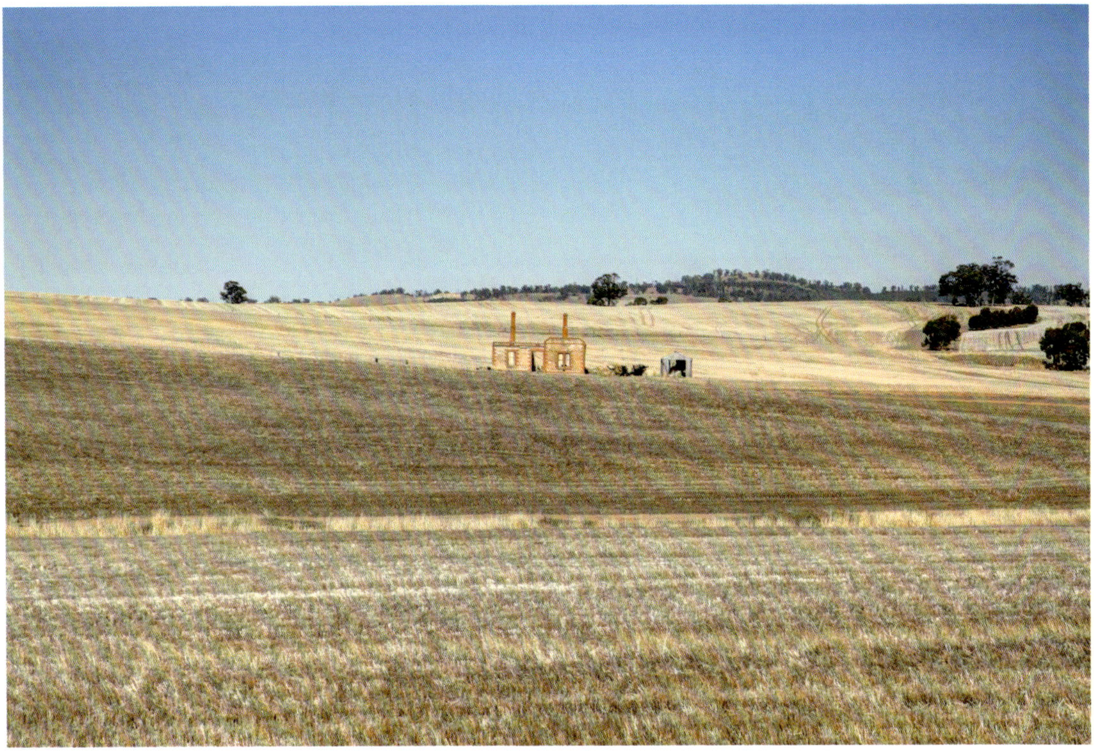

A stone ruin sits in the back paddock of a rural property.

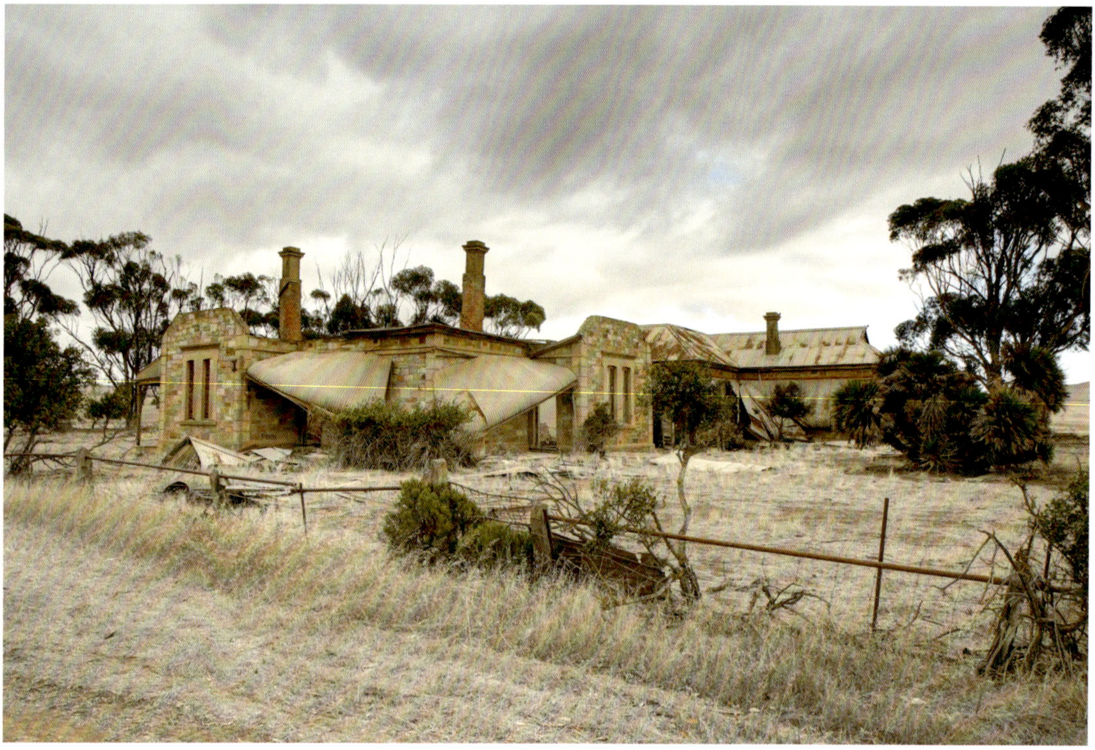

A crumbling homestead in the Eudunda region.

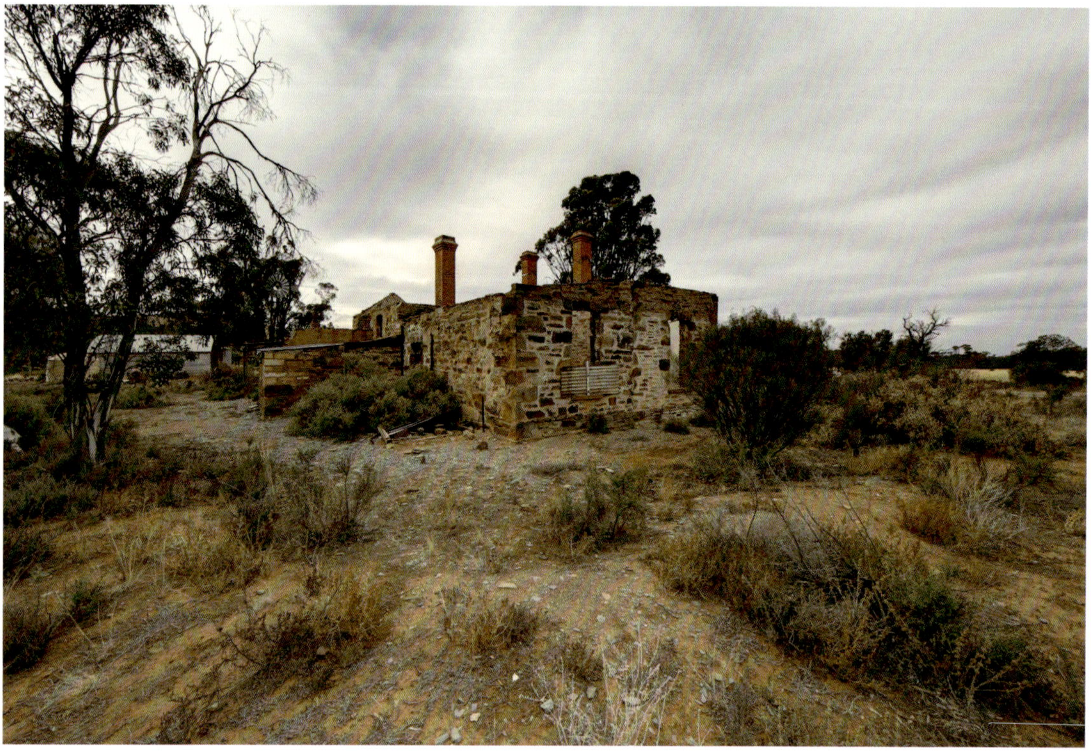

A stone ruin in the Mount Bryan region.

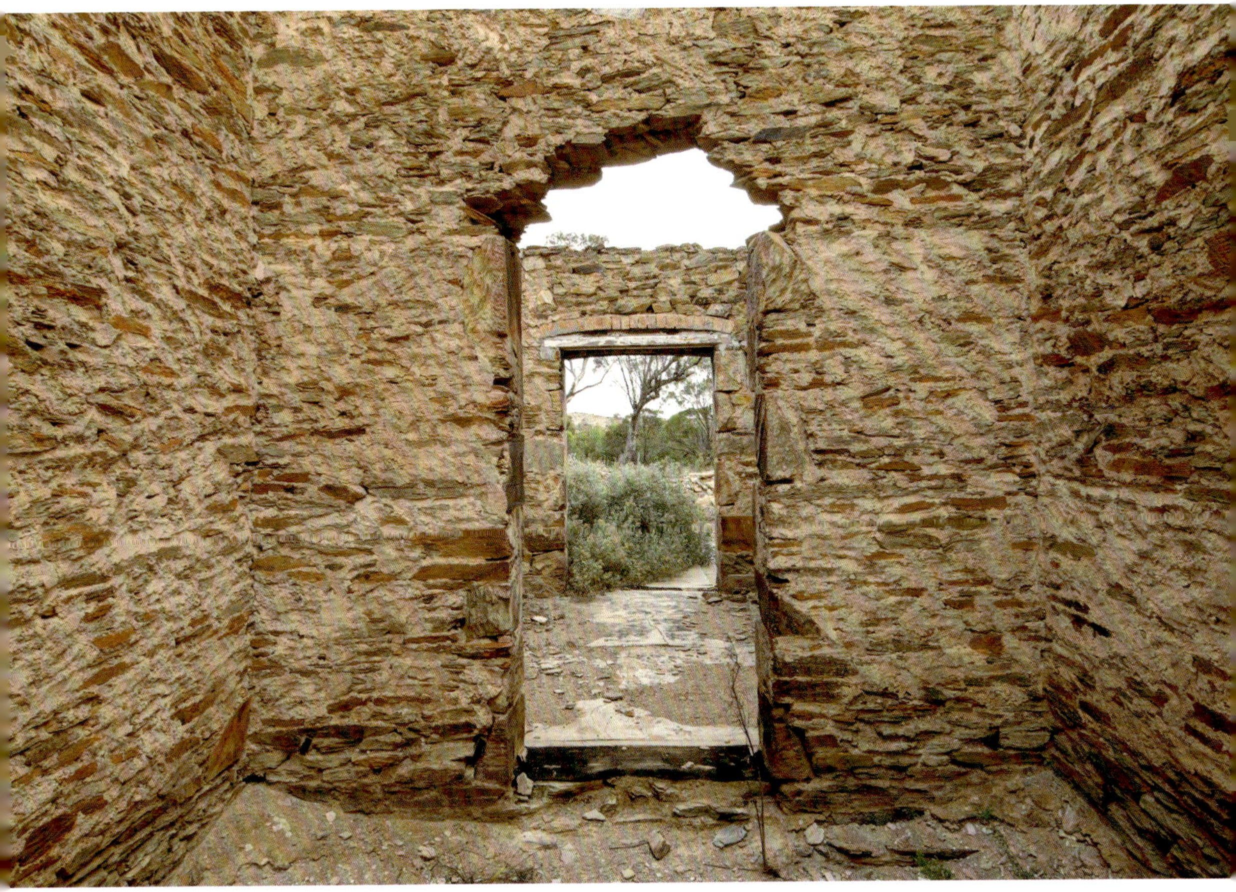

The interior of this slate stone ruin reveals the timely, intricate work involved in its construction.

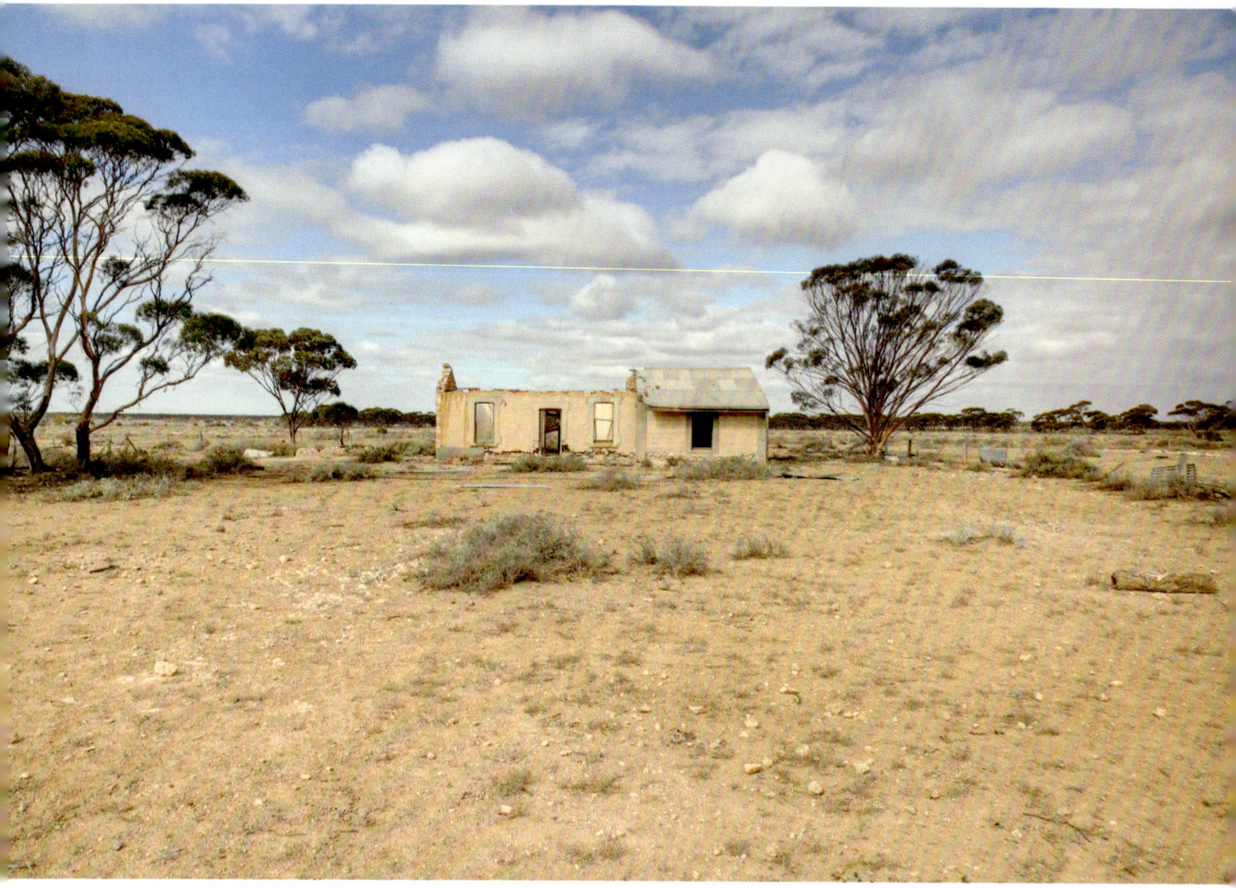

A number of farmhouse ruins dot the Brownlow landscape.

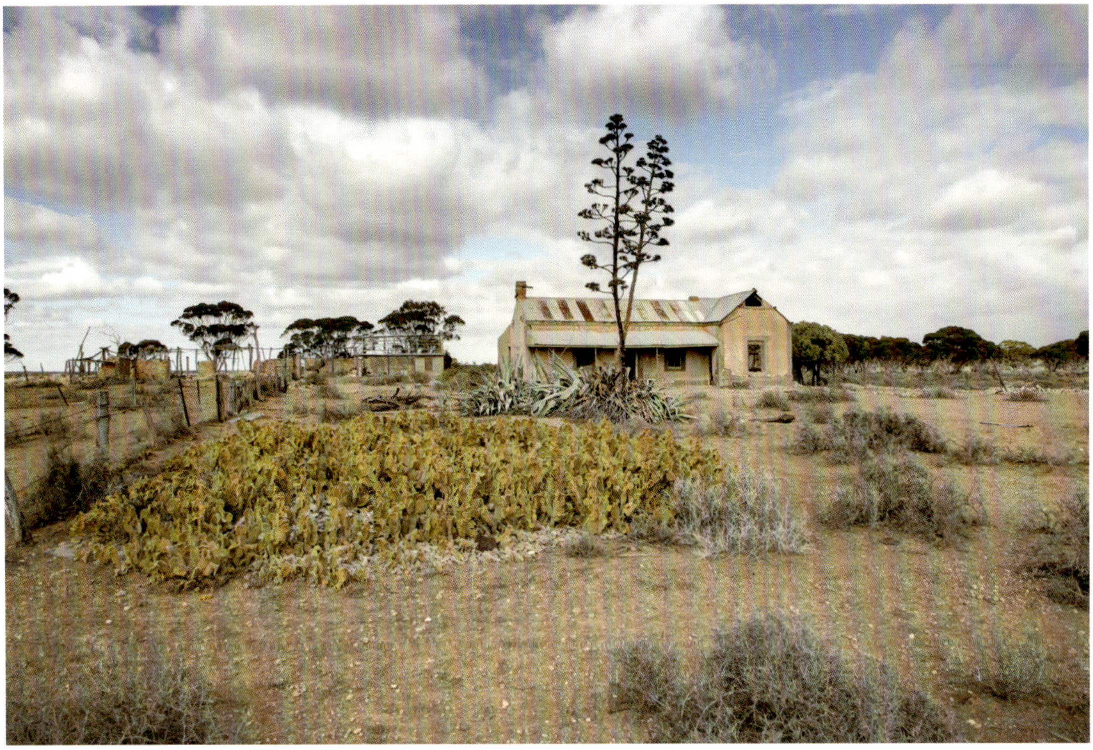

A swarm of succulent's creep slowly towards this homestead ruin near Brownlow.

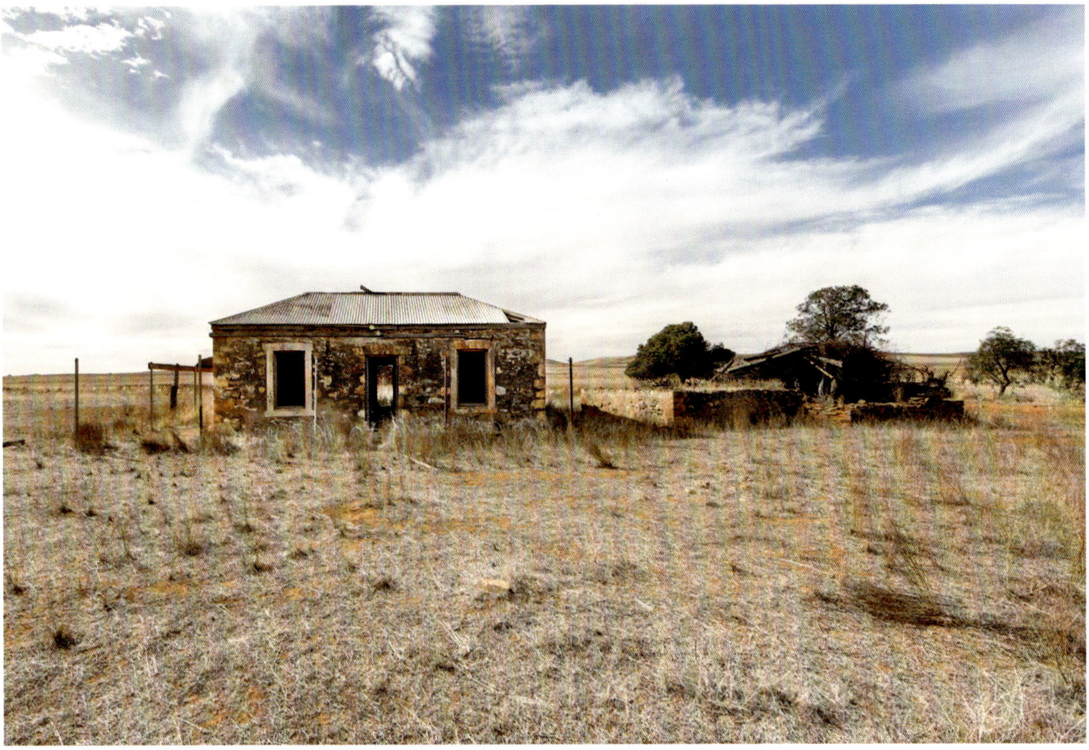

A common stone ruin in the state's mid-north.

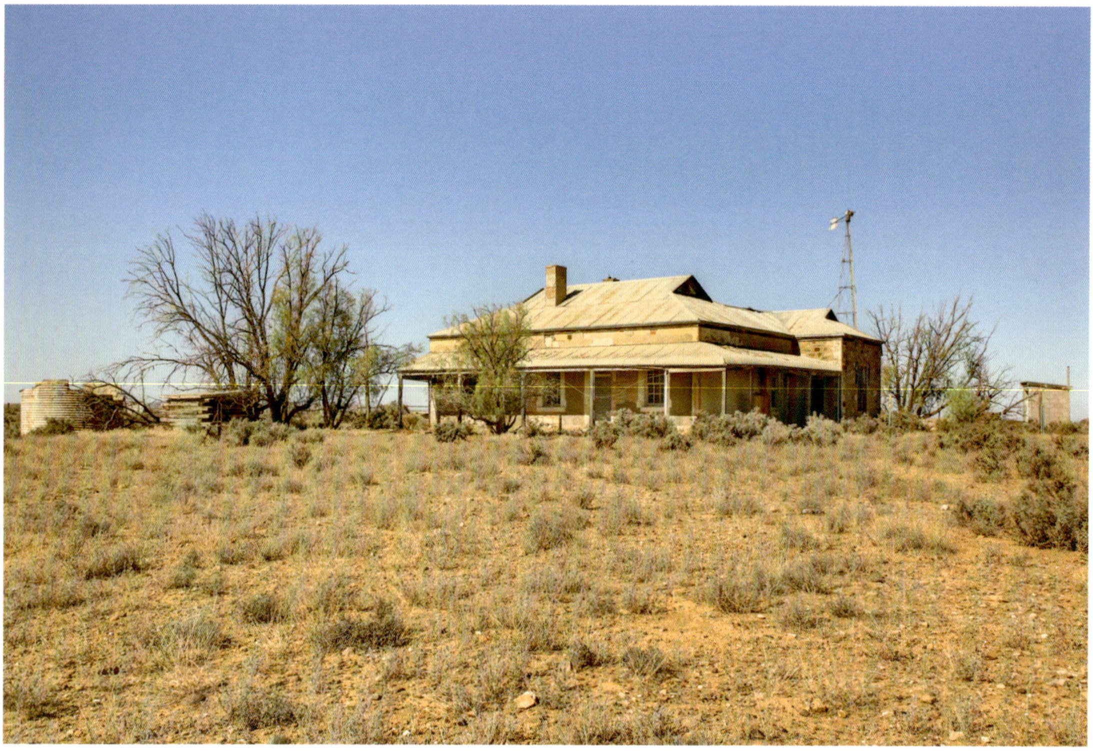

A fading desert farmhouse in the state's arid mid-northern region.

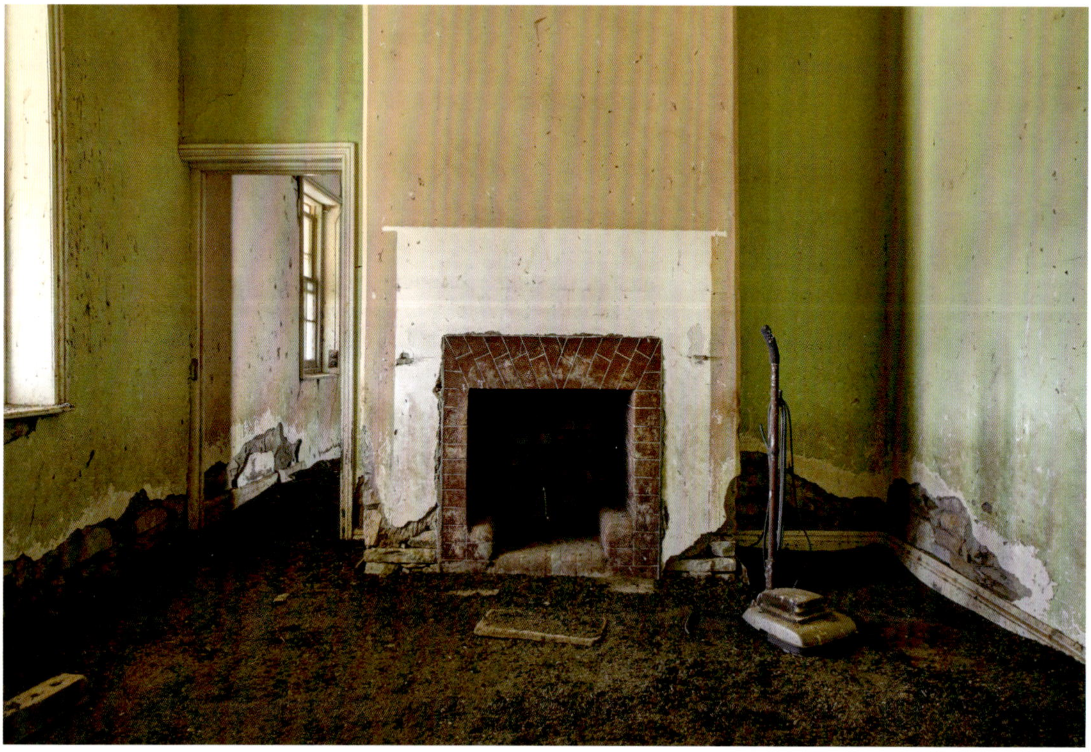

This deserted sparse interior still contains subtle hints of former domesticity.

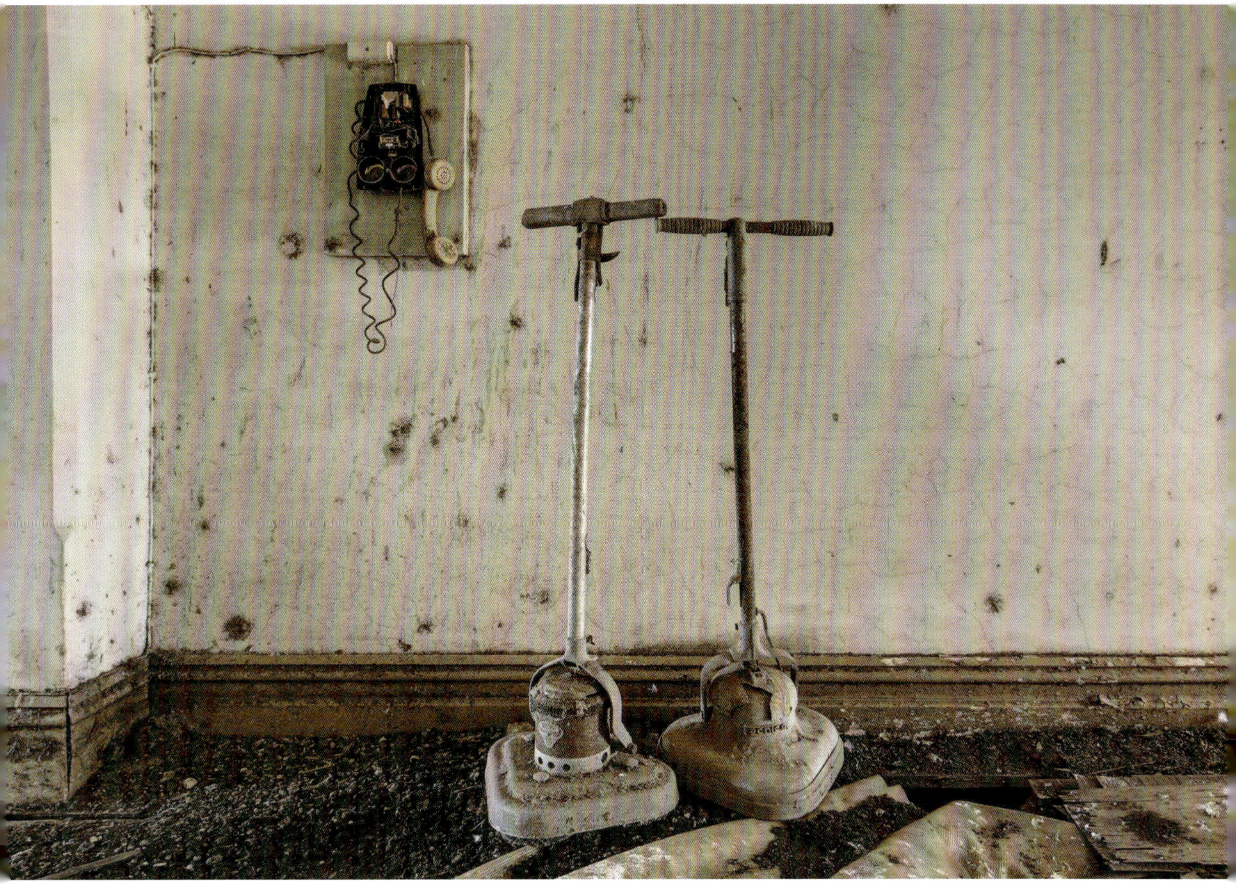

Two vintage vacuum cleaners standing dormant in a hallway filled with pigeon faeces.

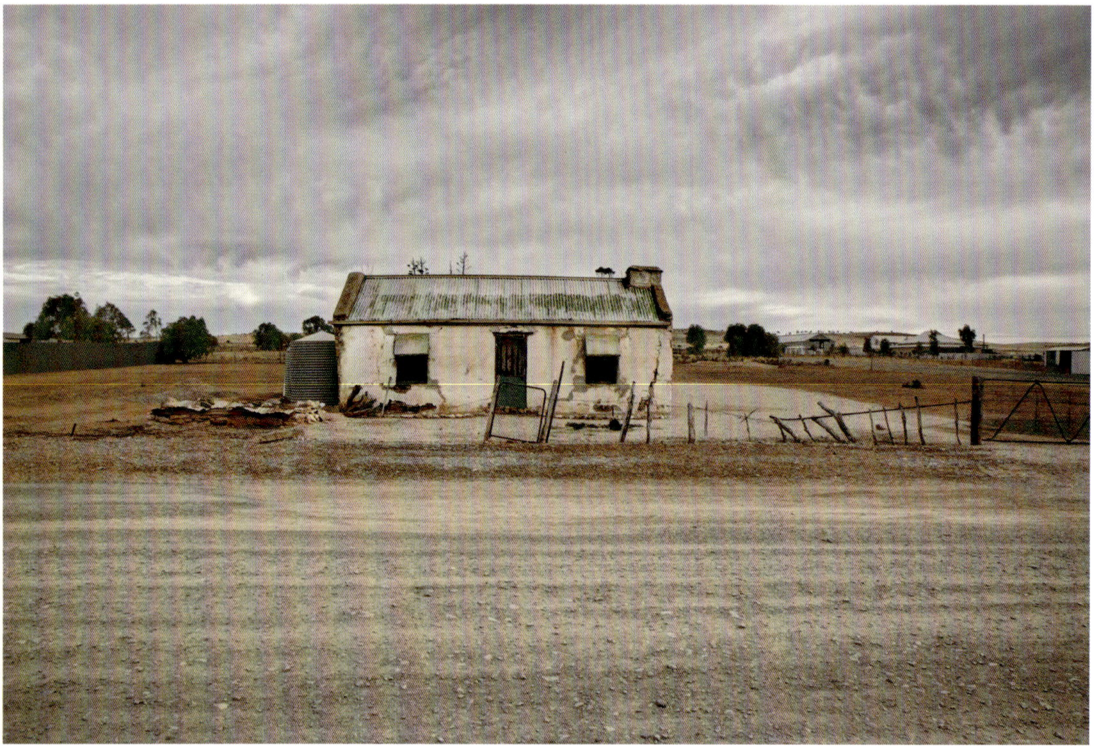

A number of dilapidated ruins dot the landscape in the historic township of Terowie in the state's mid-north.

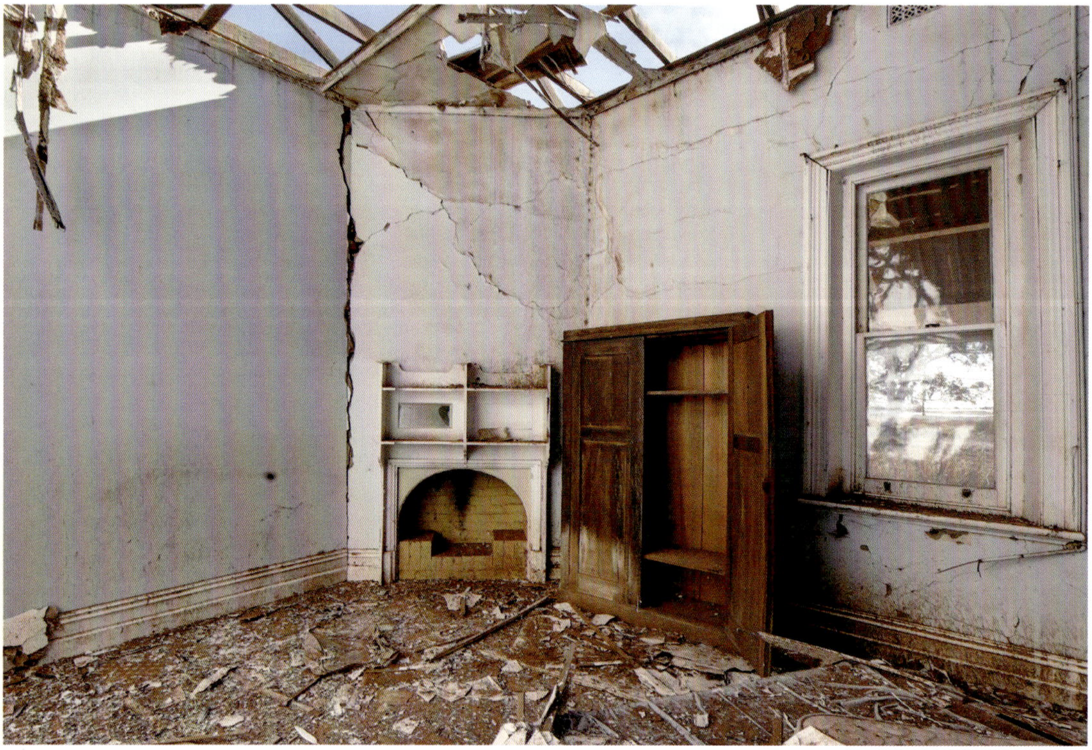

A former bedroom in a now derelict farmhouse.

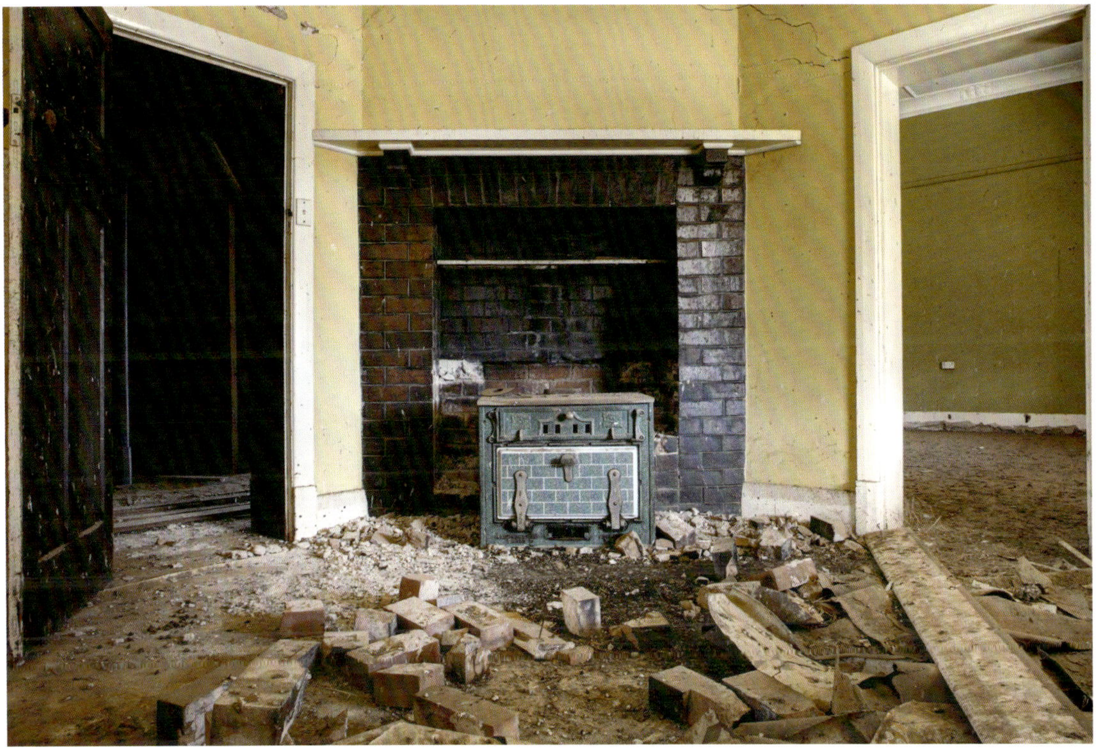

Wood-fired stoves and ovens are usually the only remaining original feature inside these now derelict kitchens.

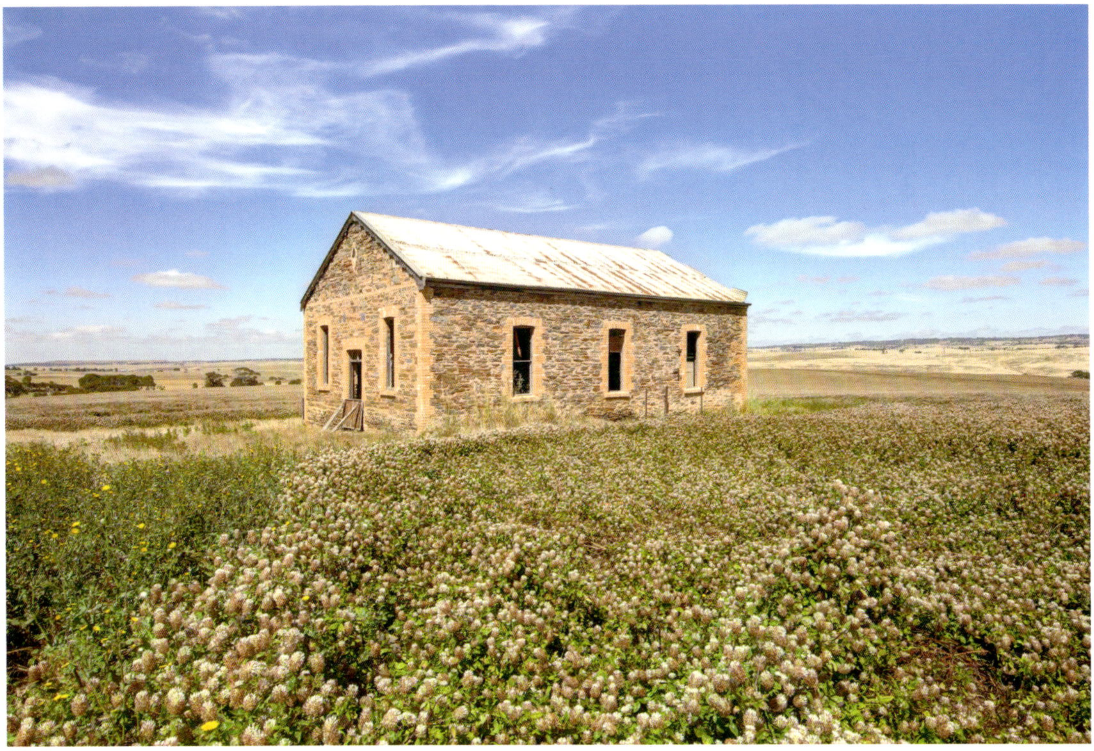

The Bondleigh Hall sits in a field in the picturesque Bremer Valley.

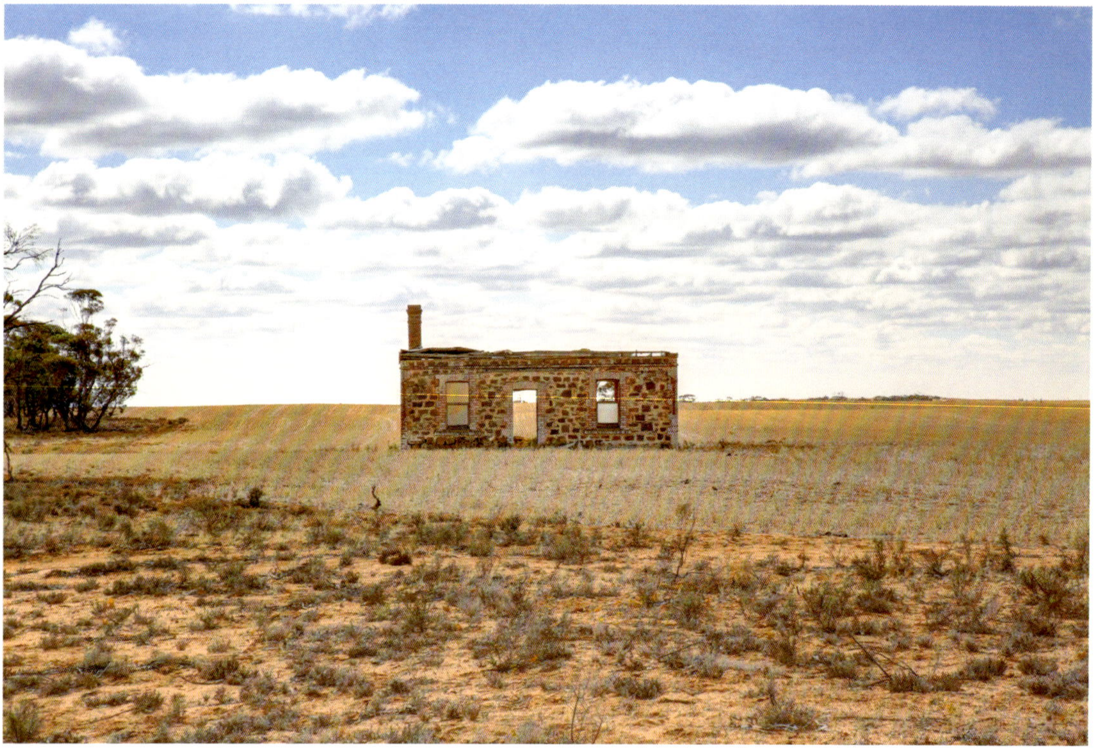

A simple stone ruin in the Loxton region.

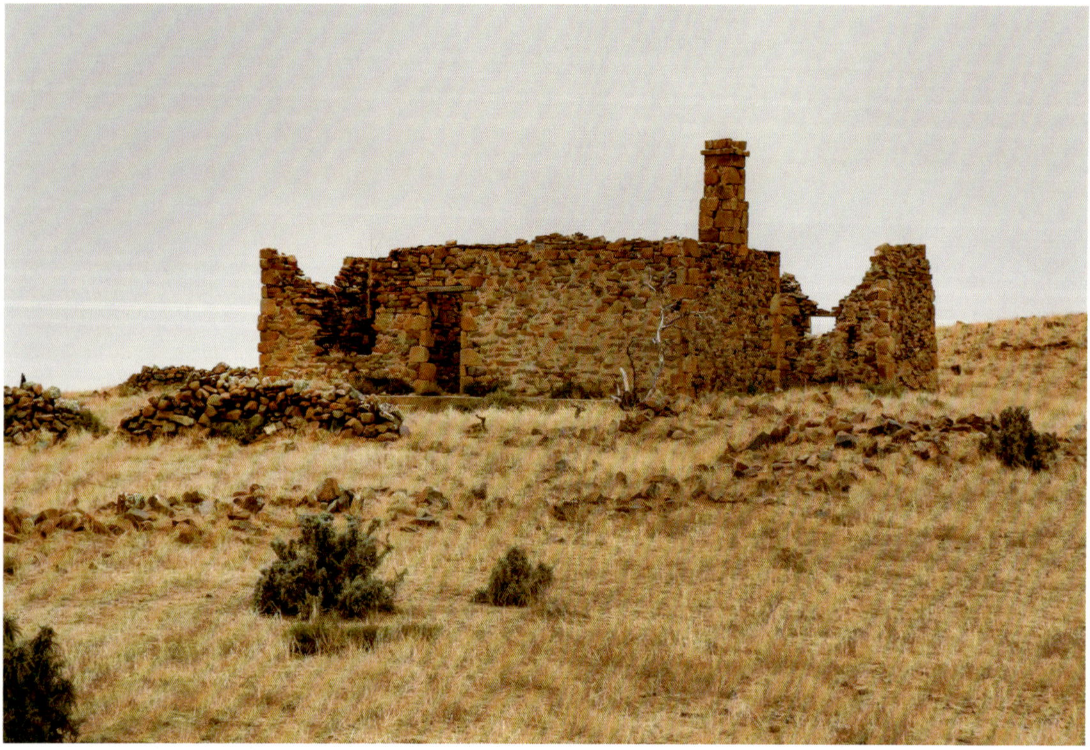

A ruin sits lonely along RM Williams Way.

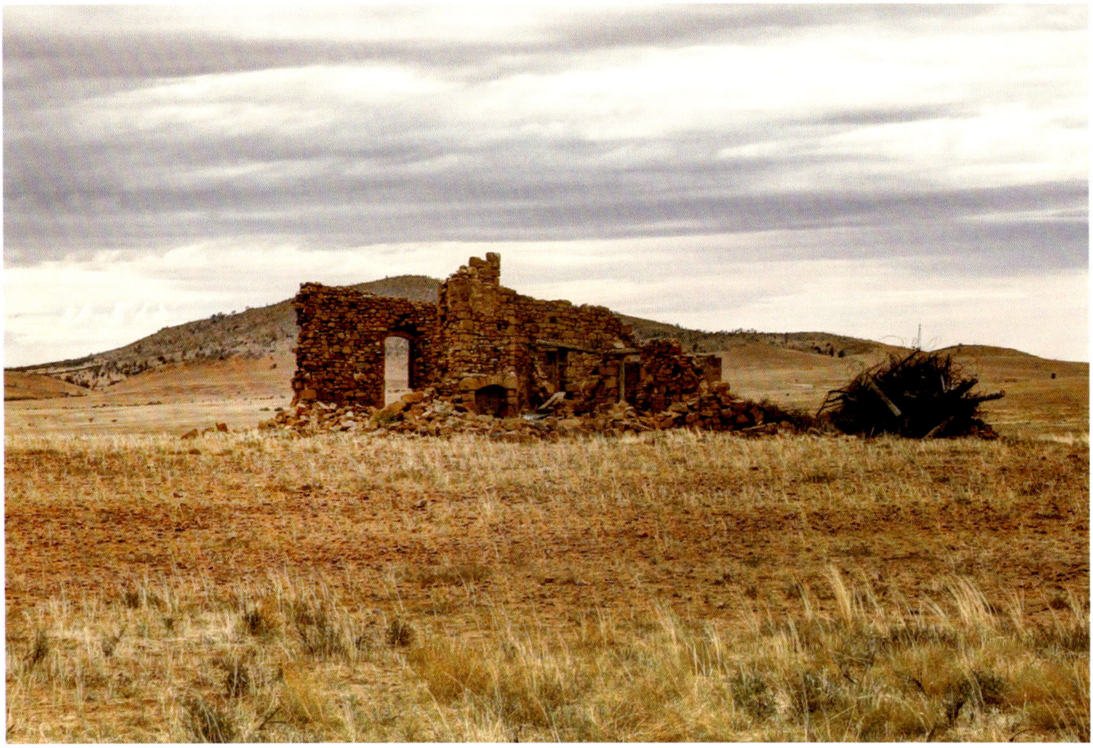

Crumbled former farmhouses are a common sight along RM Williams Way.

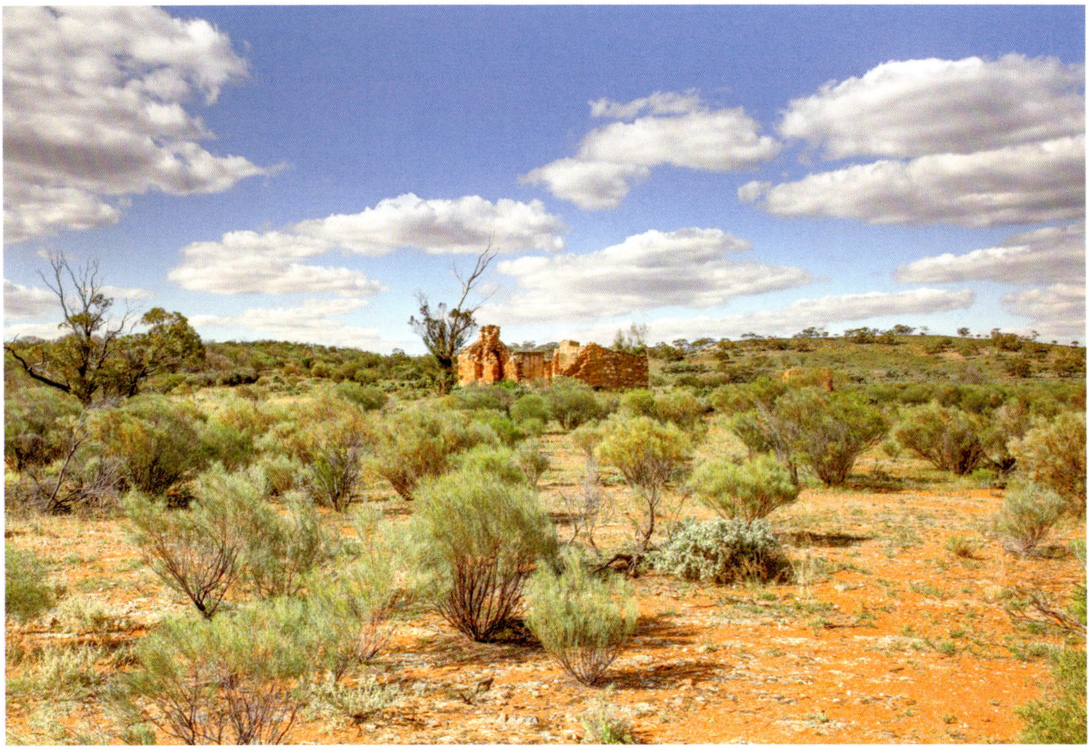

A crumbling desert ruin in the dry Wonna region.

2

DIESEL AND DUST IN BURRA

Travel 160 kilometres north from Adelaide and you will reach perhaps one of the state's most famous structural icons. A poster child for the iconic Australian rock band Midnight Oil, this derelict cottage was proudly featured on the cover of their successful 1987 album *Diesel and Dust*.

Standing lonely on the Burra Highway, the dilapidated farmhouse is a very simple four-walled stone hut, yet its uniqueness lies in the nuanced visual narrative that unfolds depending on the season. In South Australia's winter months, its lush, green surrounding fields speak of fruitful crops birthed from bountiful plains. Starkly contrasted during the region's dry summer months, the shack struggles to breathe as temperatures soar and mirage-like vapour engulfs its baking bricks.

Visited by hundreds, if not thousands, of people each year, this charming building is one of Australia's most photographed ruins.

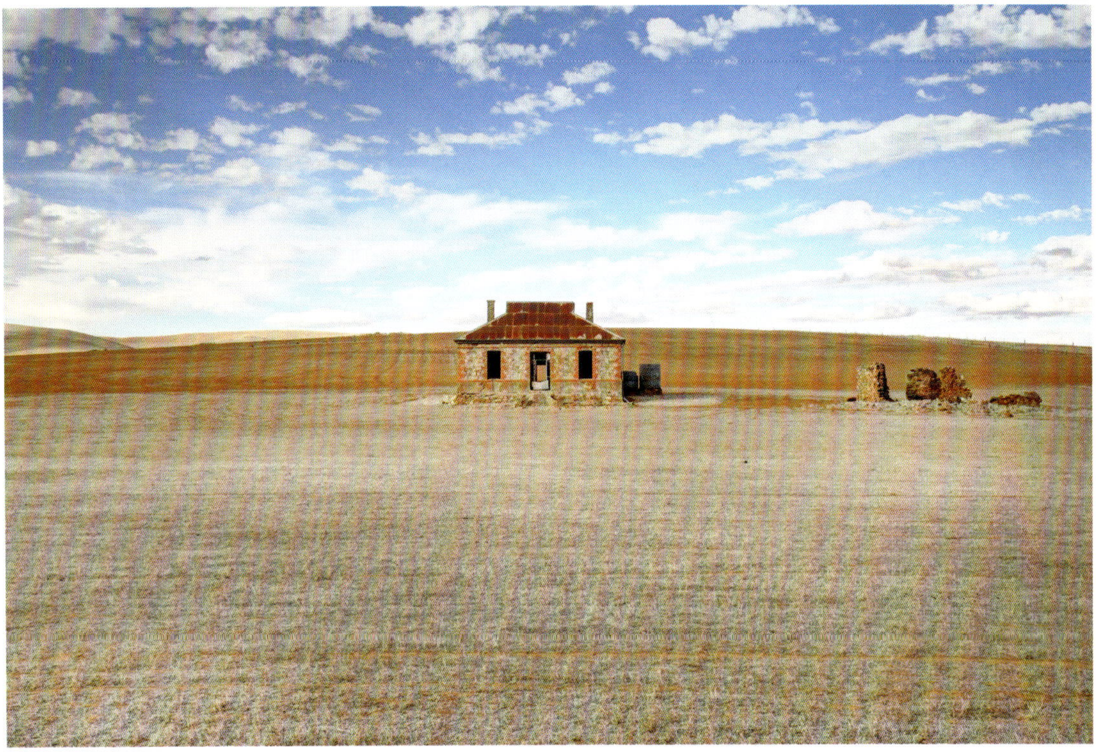

The infamous 'Diesel and Dust' house near Burra.

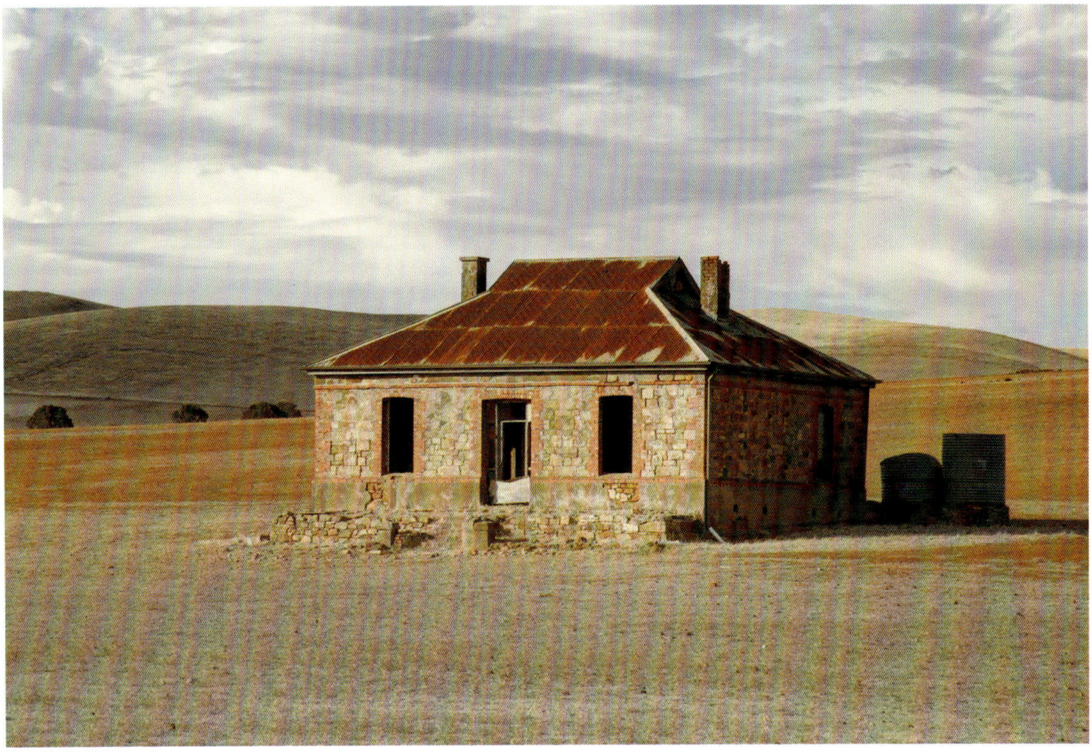

3

ABANDONED SCHOOLS

Dust steps in for what was once chalk, covering a blackboard on the wall, clinging to it in random patterns, unlike the deliberate letters and numerals created by steady, patient hands years before. The yellow and red lint of time instead coats the interiors within these once lively and noisy spaces of abandoned schools, now obscuring windows once clear and oft stared out of by bored students dreaming of the lunch bell's ring. The sounds of occasional birds are the only ringing noises these days, but—much like the timetable of maths, English, history, lunch—these birds have strict routines, too.

An old bicycle rusts outside, now outgrown and long forgotten by its owner. Trees that once stood lushly and dizzily, as children played around their perimeters, are now browned and arid, no longer fed from the running of the schoolyard bubbler. This bubbler, once clad to by thirsty mouths, now has a layer of leaves and rain water shallowly covering its old, metal belly.

This once noisy place of learning is in silent meditation—and has been for years.

Within the classrooms themselves, the remnants of alphabet guides are stuck to the wall like a reminder that when all else crumbles, words still remain. When there is no reason and disorder prevails, the shapes of the alphabet remain constant. The wonky A and D and J presciently provide what soothes us, when we feel abandoned and alone ourselves.

The halls once flush with busy children rushing here and there are quiet. Authoritative figures, once strolling the halls with hands clasped behind their back, casting a spell of command over their younger fledglings, guiding them through parabolas and adverbs and periodic tables, have departed.

Faded outlines of four squares drawn in white lines on asphalt are a reminder of games rendered simple yet important, with the need of only a tennis ball. The rapt attention of ten children would only be shattered by the sound of the bell heralding the start of class. Years of rain and dirt and mud have obscured any games of hangman or nought and crosses once drawn in the dust next to the oval.

The bench is rotted now, and one leg has fallen away totally; no one to sit and no one to hold.

Derelict schools provide us with nostalgia unlike any other structures: they take us back to the confusion and agonies, the joy and lightness of being young.

If you listen closely, the spaces echo with the laughter and gossip we once embroiled ourselves in. Lockers line deserted halls, reminding us of friendships grown and friendships lost, notes slipped to crushes, teenagers sneaking off to dark spots. Empty classrooms are scattered with papers, among the dereliction.

Schools live on in our memories—good or bad—be they still running, knocked down, or left to decay. Just like the letters on the wall, our formative years of education are indelibly imprinted in our minds, too.

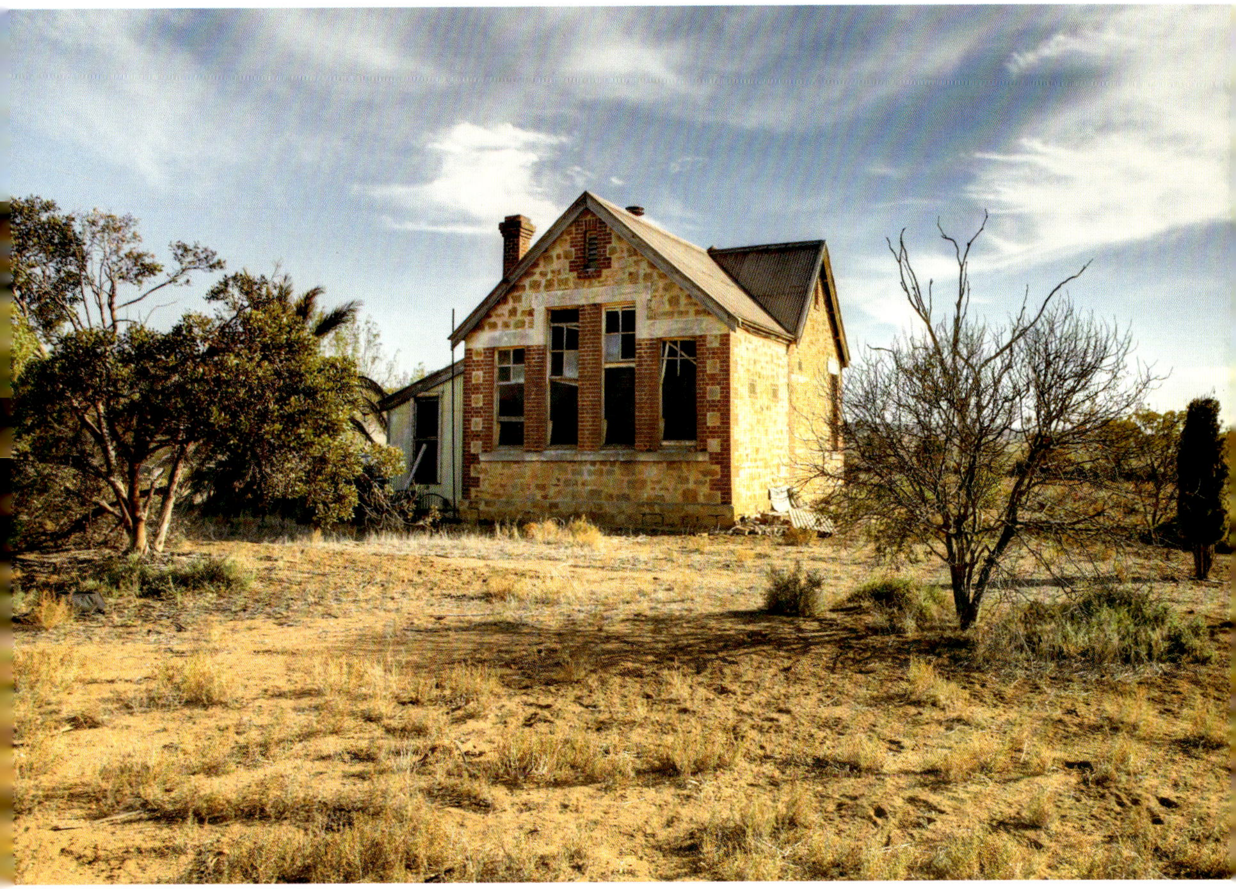

A classic rural school in South Australia's northern region.

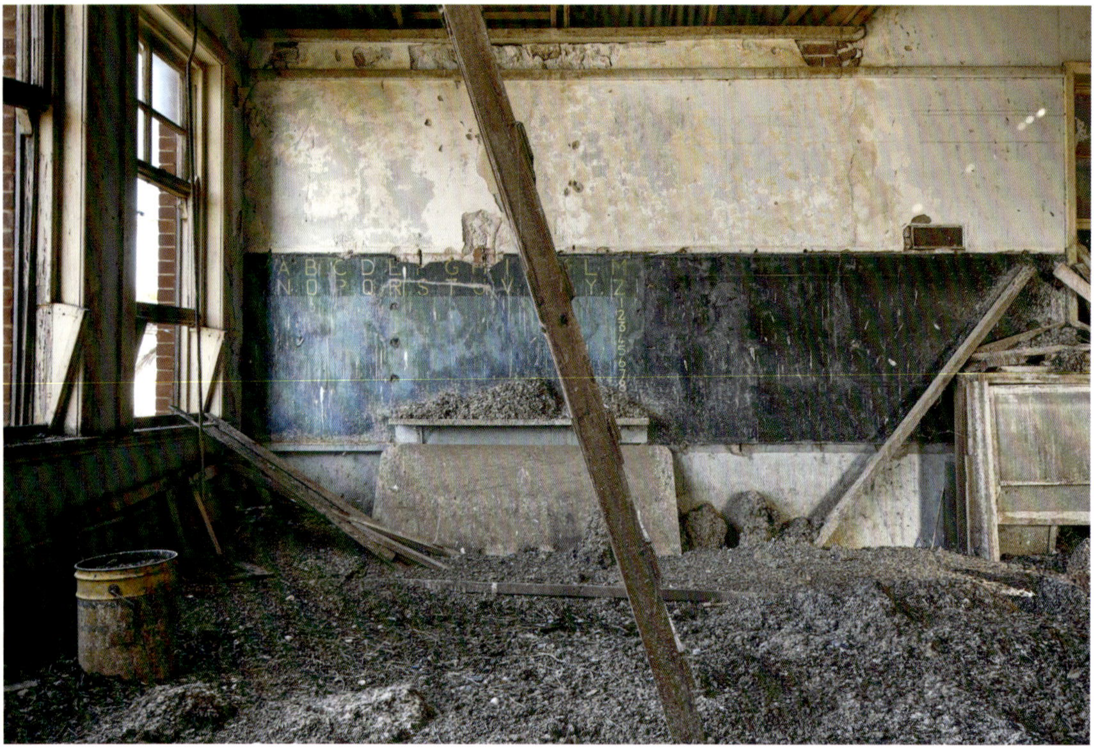

Filled with years of pigeon faeces, some features of the classroom's original interior are still intact.

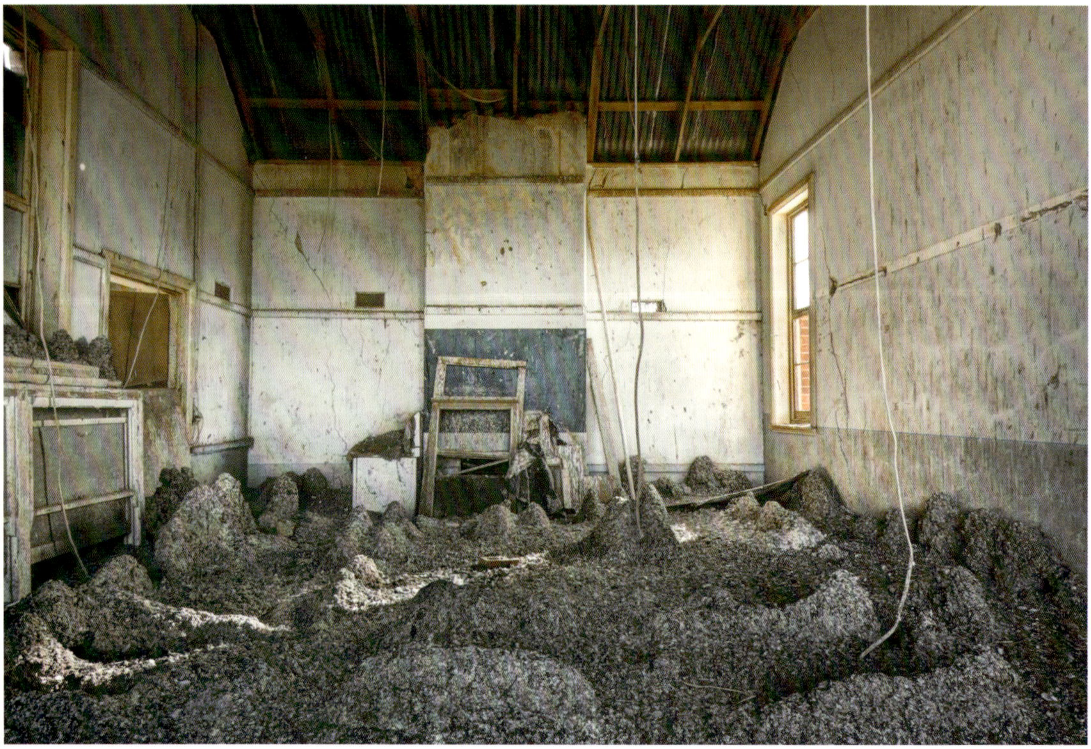

Piles of pigeon faeces make this interior a relatively hazardous space.

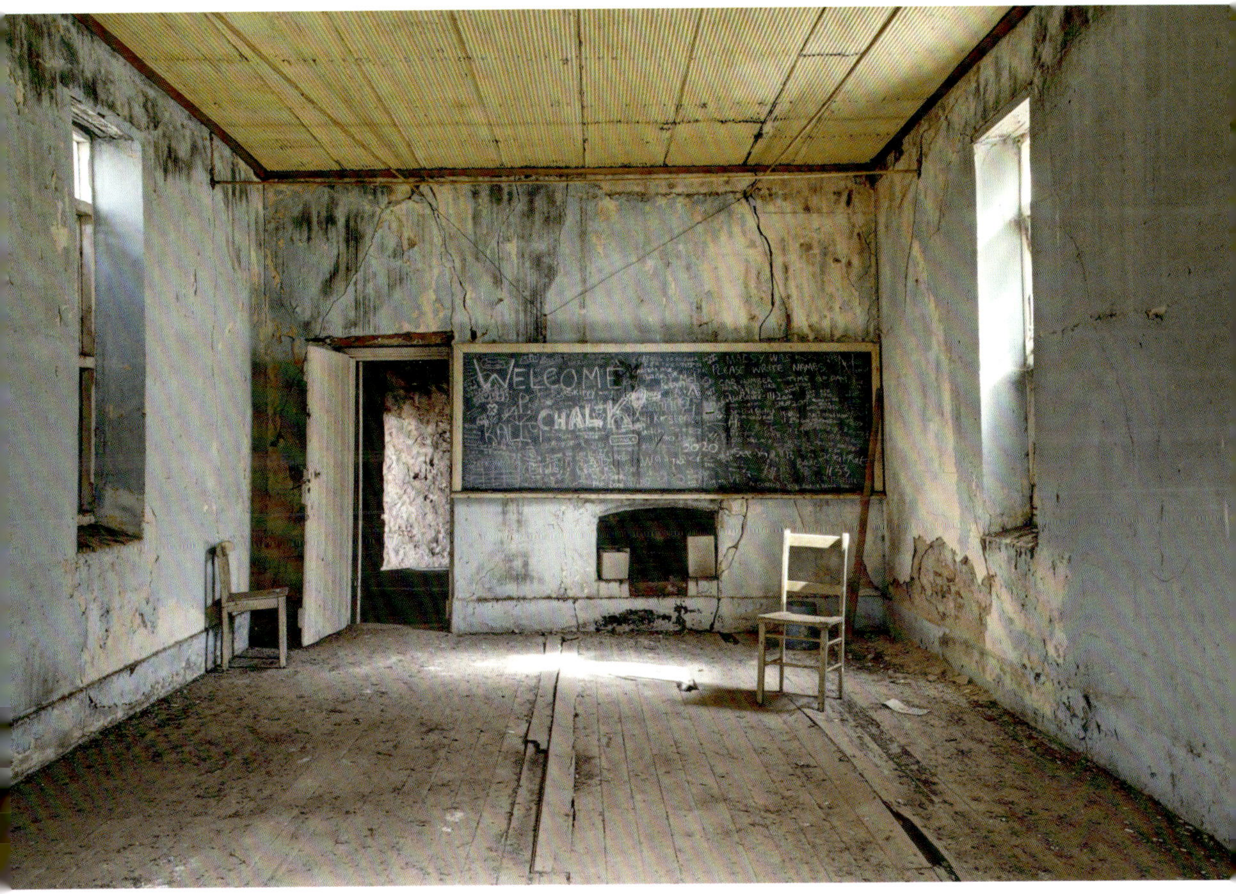

Scrawled names on the blackboard are often left by campers and road-trippers who have visited this discarded school.

4

PUZZLE PARK

This abandoned water park, opened in 1985, was once a huge pull for South Australia, consistently bringing in visitor numbers to make it decisively a central tourist destination for the area. It was also definitively era-distinctive, a period of time captured by curly slides, giant rocking giraffes and go-karts—the sort of family fun park that hits you with a jolt of nostalgia upon thinking back on your visits as a child.

But now, only eeriness floods a park once full of water, aridity drowning the solo visitor with an encompassing feeling of dehydration. But in this abandoned space, there are places where nature has won. Vines take over the picnic spaces in triumph, and reclaim a man-made environment in their supple green grip. And, on green: swamps take the place of the once blue, chlorinated pools that children would land in with a splash. Water is not being displaced by rapidly moving children anymore, it sits stagnant at the feet of cracked slides, as if waiting to envelop the slippery dip itself when it eventually topples into the weeds and mud. The swamp mirrors the stasis of the park now. Nothing runs here anymore: no children and no water.

It once boasted Australia's largest maze, and many of its rides—such as the 90-metre waterslide and the huge flying fox—were not for the faint of heart. The water parks signs boasted bright colours accompanied by an atmosphere of carefree excitement. It was a raucous place, loud with splashes and screams.

A blue slide stands in the north corner, its once fecund belly now dry and roasting in the sun, fading to a dull shade of what was a vibrant, sunny hue. A dusty summer sheen now lies over it, telling a story of former glory, small tales of joy via the shrieks of many children. Its interior, protected and kept watered, weathered the bumps and prongs from the pointiest elbows, as children screeched down its slick insides and arrived at the bottom in a splash that heralds the pinnacle of joy without gravity.

That gravity, however, ran out. While almost 100,000 people visited in its first year of operation—and up to 3,000 a day over long holiday weekends—the park's crowds dwindled in the early 2000s in favour of bigger, more modern parks in Adelaide. The cost of insurance rose, and the park was priced out of operation.

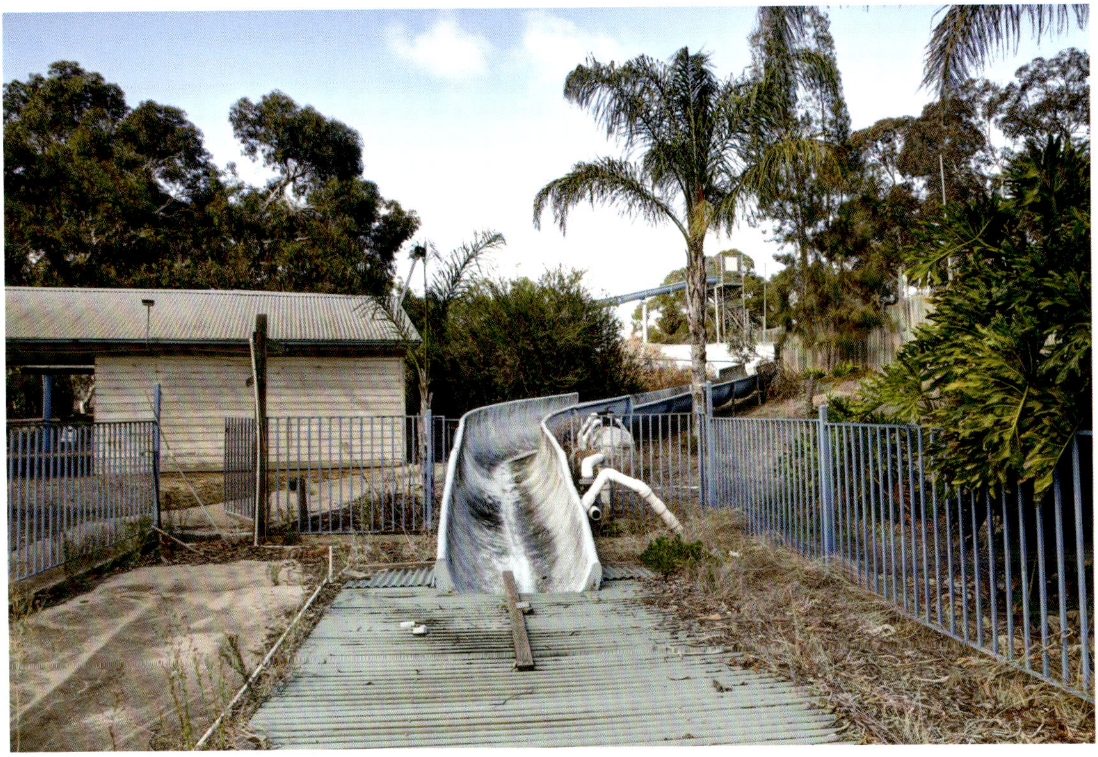

Puzzle Park's dust-covered Slippery Dip, once the establishment's centre-piece, now sits covered in dead gum leaves and dirt.

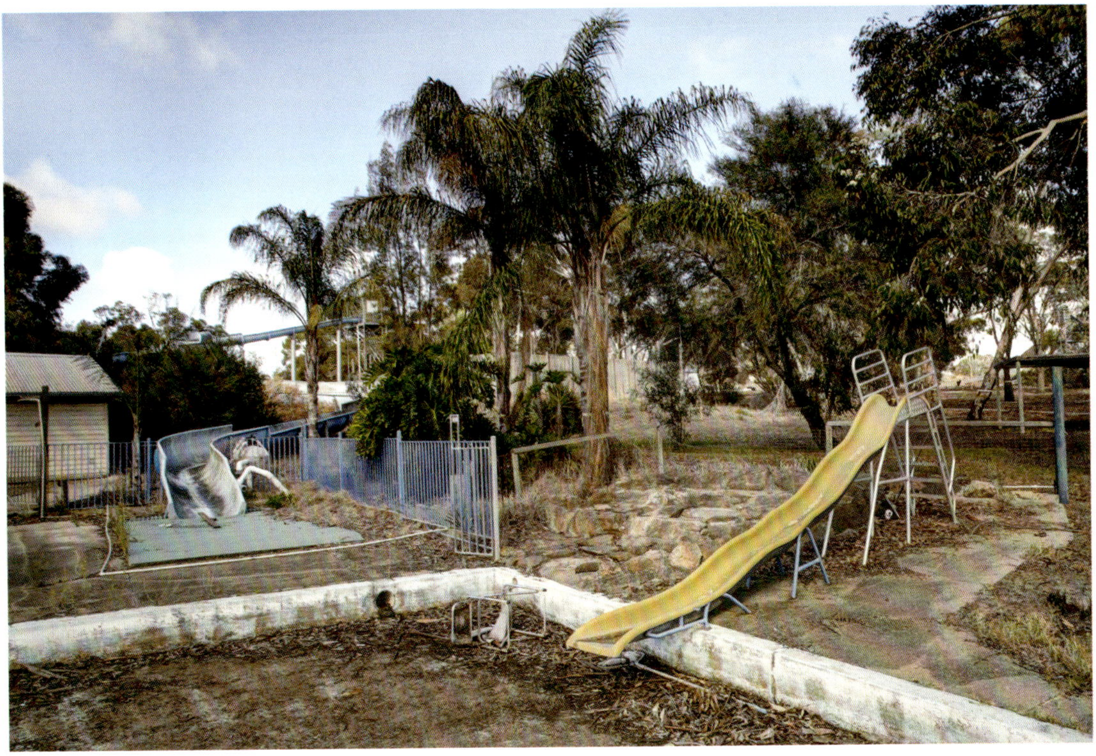

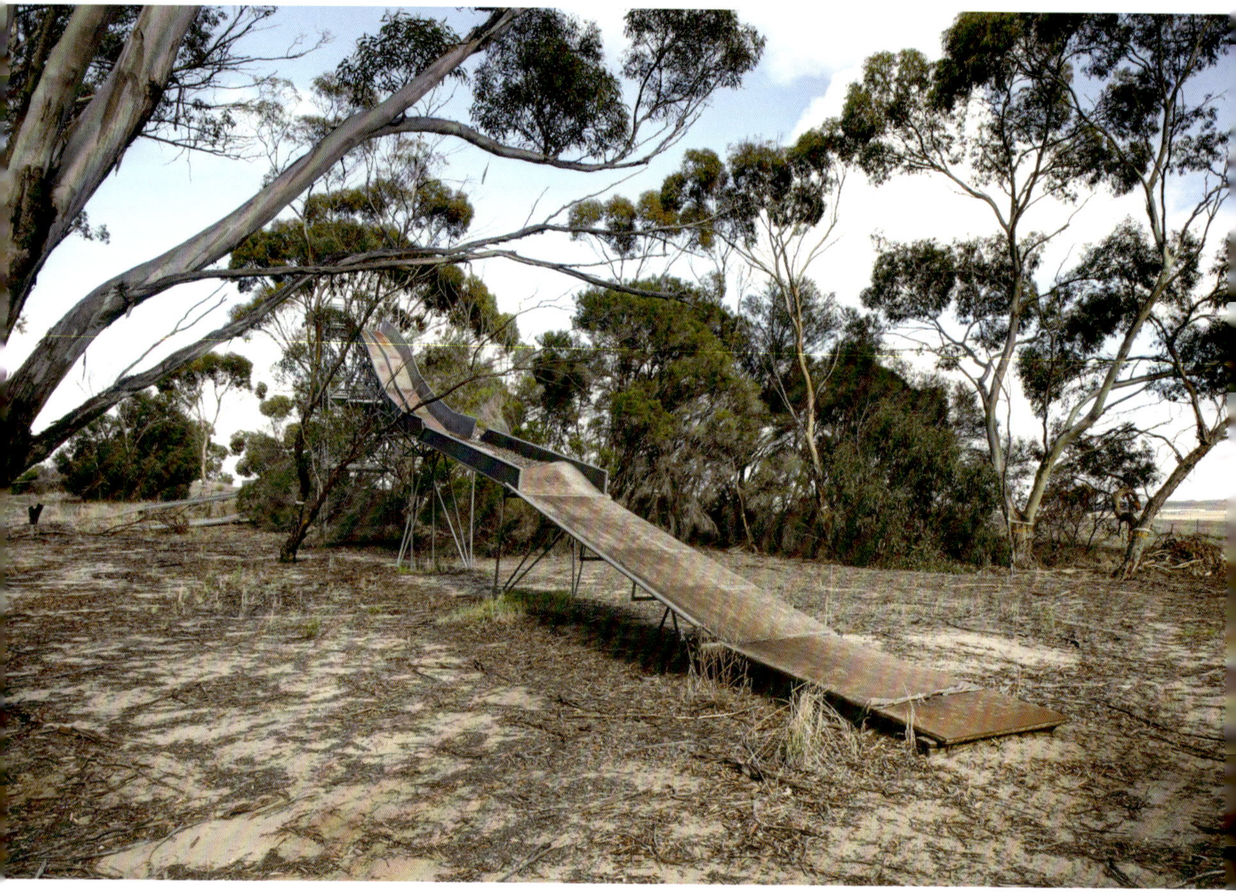

As with many abandoned places that sit silently and slowly becoming derelict, the park has over time garnered an increasing sense of impending demolition. Closed in 2007, the site was then put to auction and changed hands a few times, with buyers planning on constructing a large retirement home. However, those plans never came to fruition: in 2019, it again went up for public sale, with optimistic news articles of the time chirping 'here's your chance to own your own theme park!'

Sitting on the market for almost two years, a buyer was finally found. But though the 20-megalitre water licence comes with the park, and the sellers hoped the establishment would continue to function as a tourist attraction of some sort, the process of dismantling soon began. Another amusement space, it has been decided, is not viable, whether by way of pandemic or a changing society.

This old water park will be razed someday soon and the water will flow once again, but it will be in a very different way.

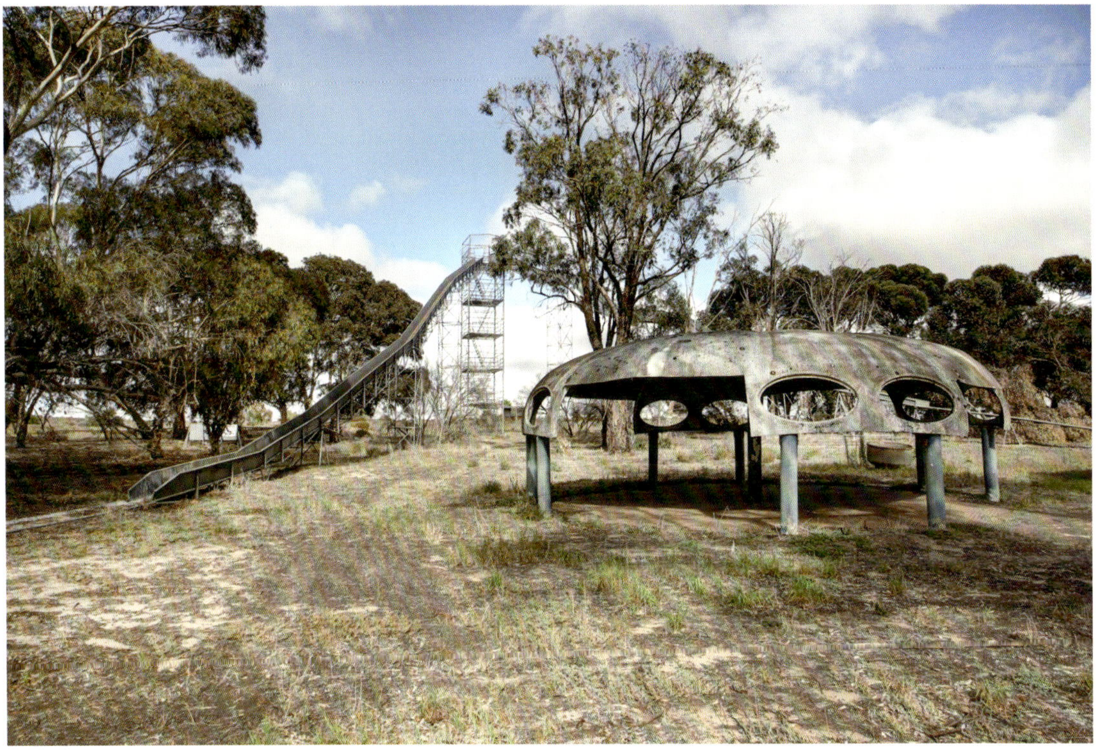

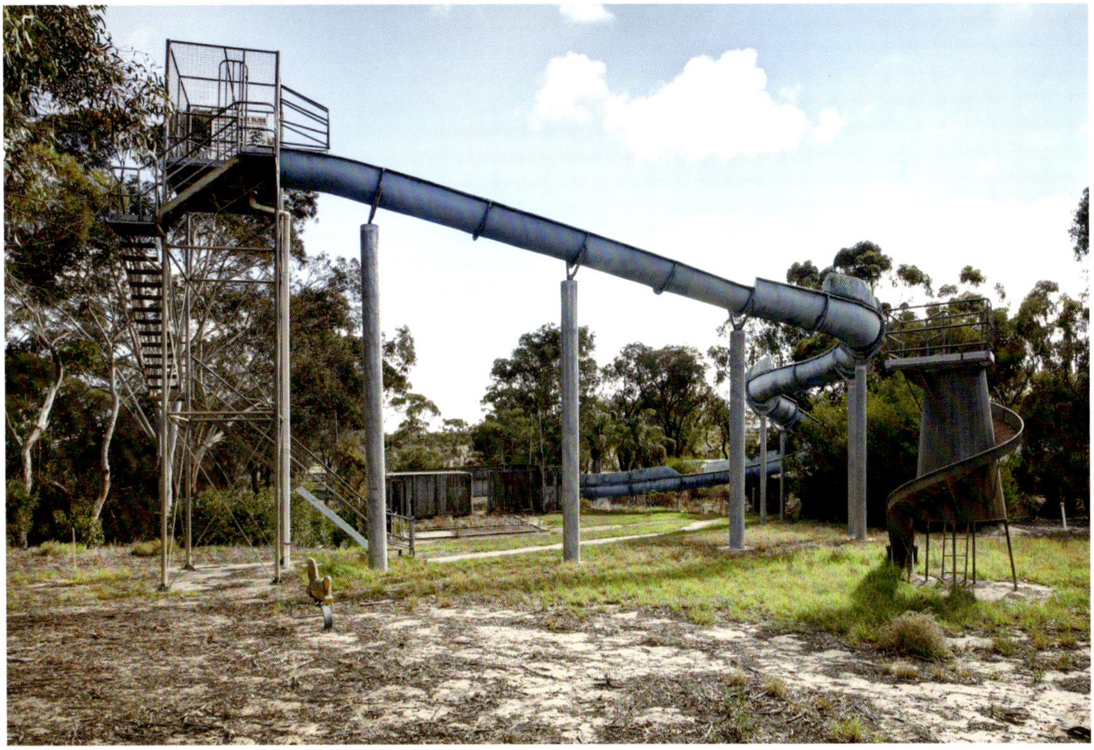

5

DERELICT TRAIN STATIONS

Train stations bring us together, bearing us aloft into our new lives, or helping us in the rituals of revisiting old ones. They provide the launching pad for adventures, or journeys spent in contemplative silence, sound-tracked by the *duh dum, duh dum* of the wheels' perpetual motion. The tracks that lead into the stations signal the unarguable, strong bars of possibility. Follow these two lines in the ground, and you can go anywhere. Be it a first trip out to the city heading south from a country home, a holiday north to warmer climates, or a one-day trip to see family back east, rising with the sun and chasing it home again. Train stations launch us onwards.

The commuters who once frequented the derelict and abandoned train stations of South Australia once stood on their platforms, eyes sleepy, stomachs full of the soup of potential adventures and dreams and loves and mistakes. Once, lukewarm sandwiches were packed and pulled out midway through journeys, a little squashed, but still full of nourishing goodness to keep the weary traveller sated.

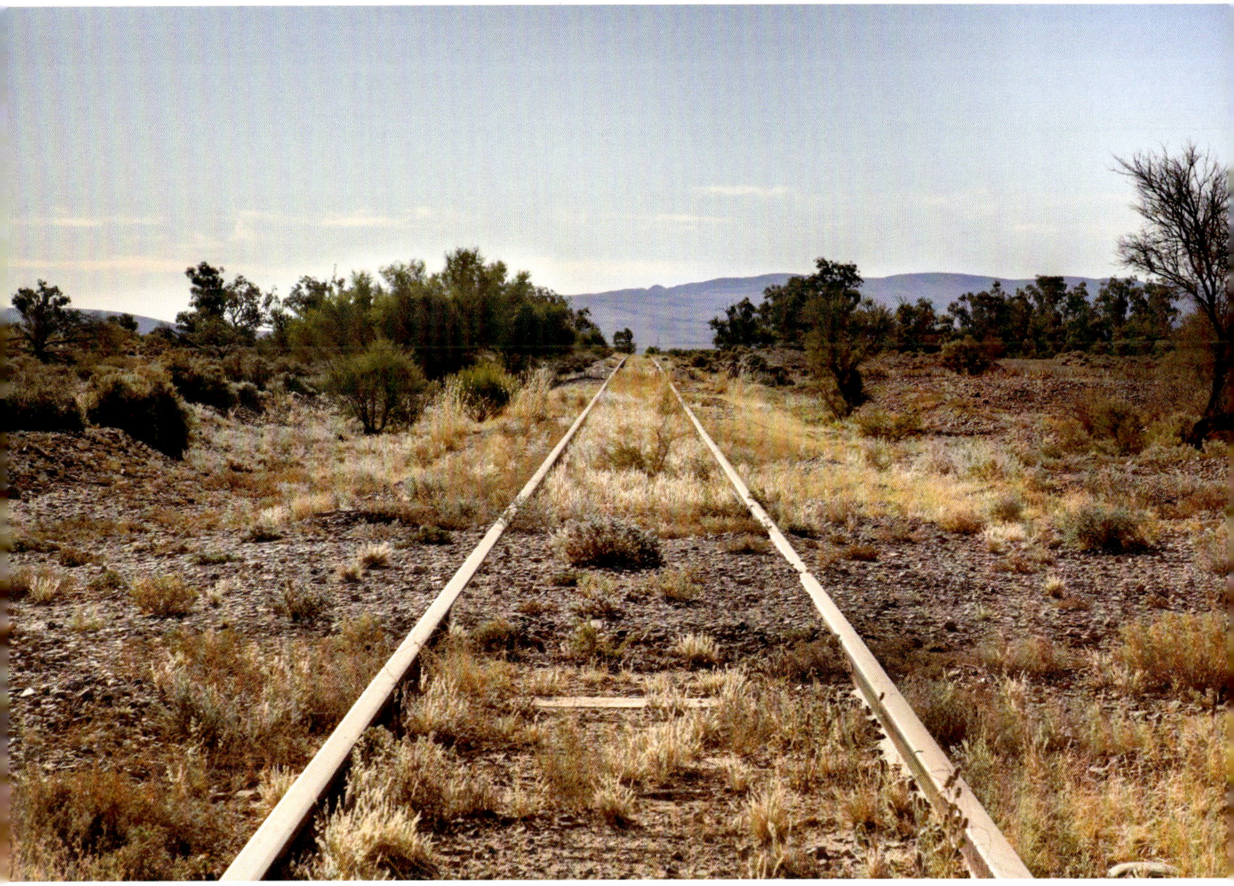

6

MANOORA STATION

Manoora is a small town a little north of Adelaide, on the Barrier Highway and within the Clare Valley. From a word that means 'a water spring' in the language of the Ngadjuri people, the town's now-abandoned rail station was originally part of the Burra railway line—a line that led the town to prosper. The line was opened in 1870, yet construction of the station itself was not completed until the century's final years. Today, the structure's exterior remains in good condition. The patterned steel trim on the awning remains intact and the attractive pattern of the red and blue brick walls still provides an engaging focal point. Two palm trees tower nearby, yet not quite impinging on this timely rail station that has been latent for some time.

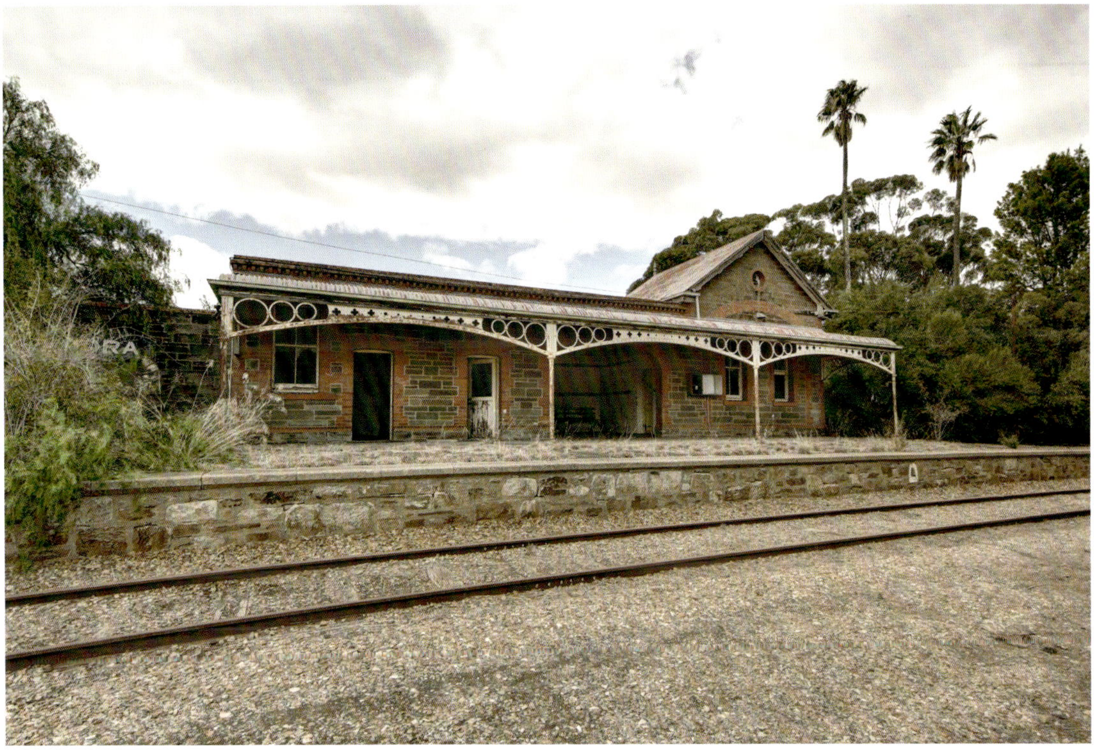

Manoora Station's classic awning still stands after many years.

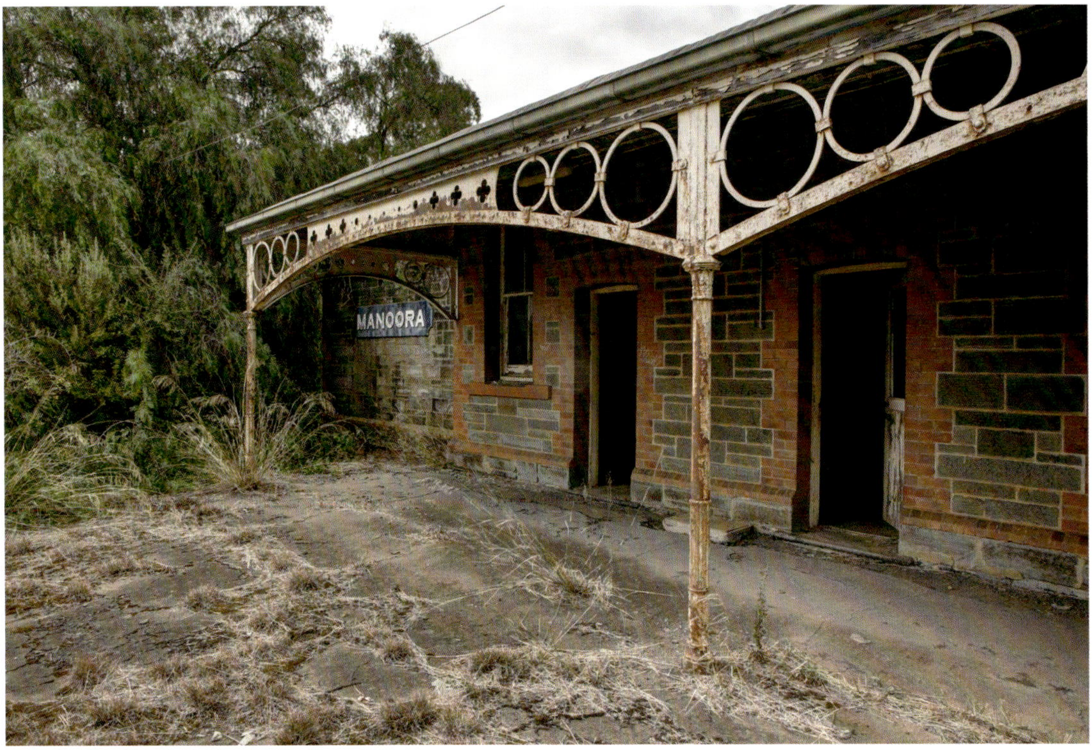

7

EUDUNDA STATION

This station today also stands silent and motionless. Built in the late 1870s when the Kapunda railway line was extended, the town—established in 1872—is 415 metres above sea level and claims its title as one of the coldest towns in South Australia during winter. The name Eudunda, in the Ngadjuri language, means 'sheltered water or spring', and indeed, the town is located near a permanent spring, an essential water supply for Eudunda in the nineteenth century.

Three identical stone building fronts populate the station, with three identically placed windows. Detritus litters the front of a once-clean platform with wire and stacked up splintered woodpiles providing an air of stagnant caution. The lights are off and nobody is home is the message here—just cold brick starting to fall. Multiple chimneys poking forth from the building, however, tell us that this was indeed once a place of warmth, a refuge for weary travellers needing a motionless seat and a still room.

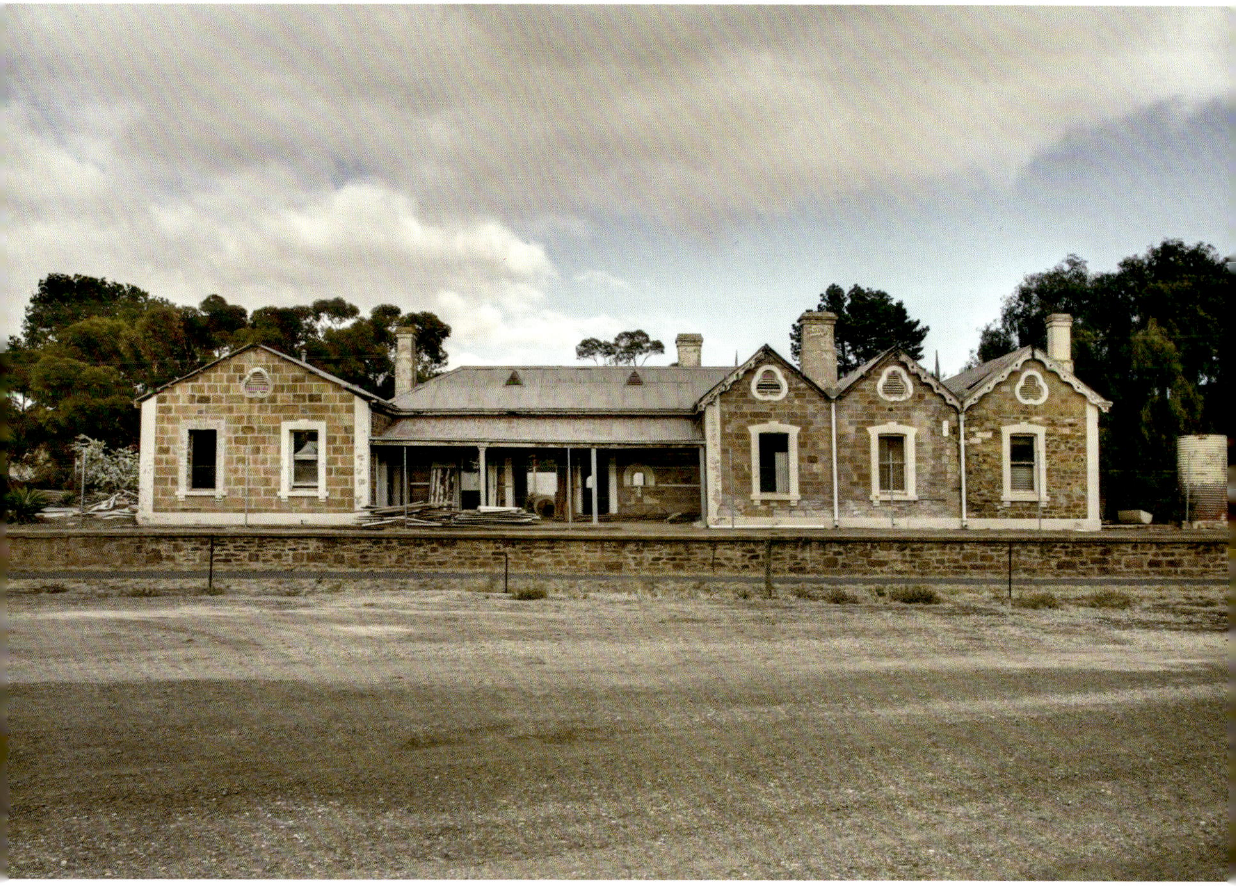

8

MERILDIN STATION

This quaint rail station is fringed by finite natural limits. Tall palm trees stand sentry, at each corner of the structure, leaning slightly towards each other as if deep in discussion on how to protect the bounty within. Red brick accoutrements add to the simple building. Other plants, even those protected from the harsh sun, are long dead. Some 145 kilometres north of Adelaide, Merildin's station was built in 1870, when the northern railway line was extended to Burra from Roseworthy, reflecting, at the time, the architectural changes crucial to the development of the railways being built throughout South Australia—connecting the state's hubs and towns.

Visitors to these sites now do not find the *da dum, da dum* or the distant hoot of an incoming train, or busy people about to be launched on to whatever journey they have laid out ahead of them that day. Instead, there are silent platforms, the only sounds being the birds and perhaps a leaf scratching across the ground as the wind gusts past. One can now step right out, beyond the platform, and on to these latent lines. Standing centred, looking onwards into a horizon where another world awaits beyond the vanishing point: a metaphor that although one journey has ended, another is yet to begin.

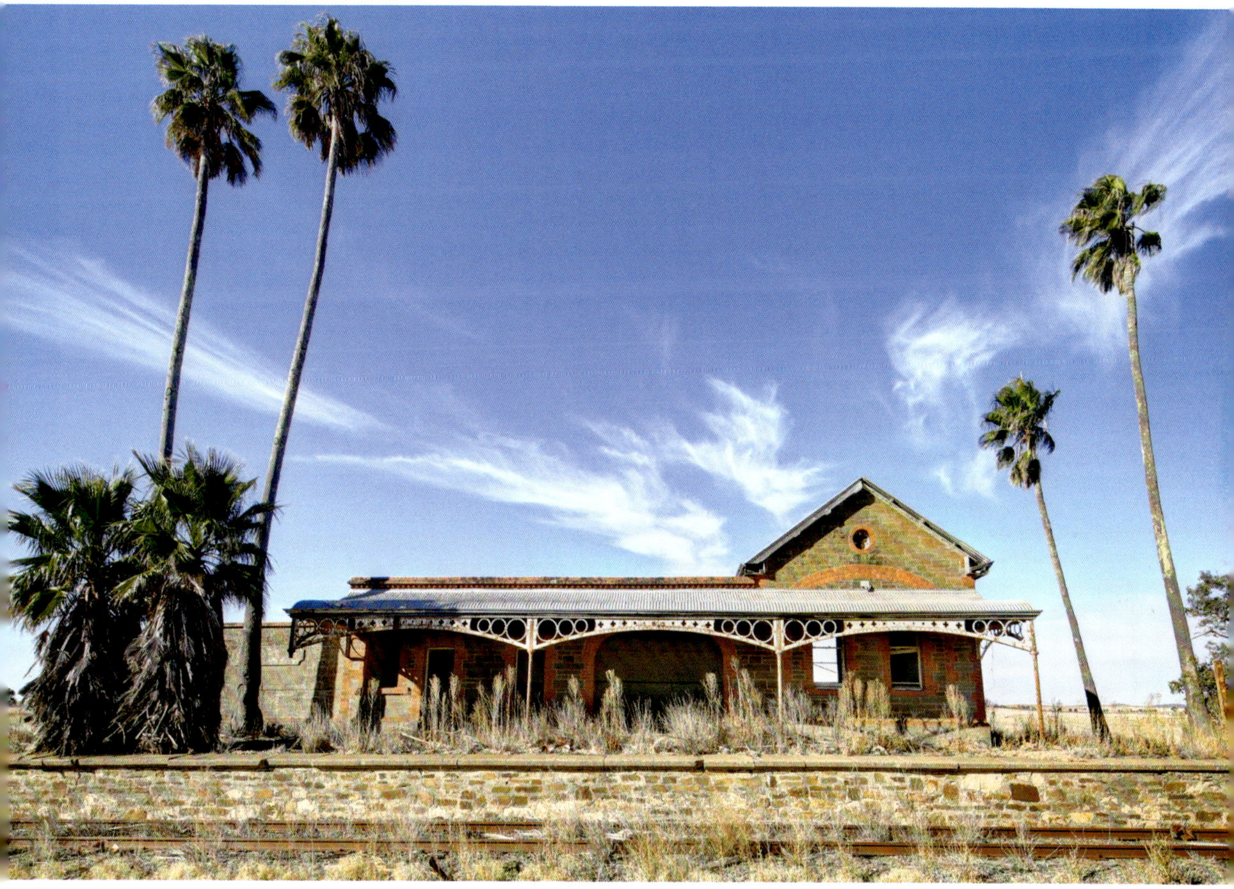

9

THE OUTBACK HIGHWAY AND THE FLINDERS RANGES

How long do the highways of South Australia stretch? How long can asphalt be painted before it turns to dust? How many hours can you drive, how many trees can you count? How many headlights beam back at you, rolling with purpose into the places you've just left?

None of these questions have definitive answers apart from perhaps 'long', 'many'.

South Australia's Outback Highway is the road from Hawker, running through Leigh Creek to Marree. The passage is some 272 kilometres long, running from its southern end in the Flinders Ranges' hub, Hawker, through Leigh Creek and its huge open-cut coal mine, and Lyndhurst and Farina. Then, onward, to the road's northern finale in Marree, a known sheep and cattle station service centre for the area. On a map, the Outback Highway traces almost straight up and down, a score in the paper.

Sandstone ruins dot the landscape as it whizzes past the passenger who is staring out the car window: punctuating long stretches of red and brown with their crumbling facades; brick becoming dirt, blending into dry ground baking in the sun.

At first glance, they seem as temples upon desert hilltops; base structures with simple geometry—all that is left—some windows, some walls, often no roofs. Who is paying their respects, at these lonely and abandoned cathedrals of dust? What were the last words spoken within them, and to which ghosts?

Within these meditative spaces—resistant to all noise, yet not weather—stand remnants of existences that were. If one were to pause, instead of rolling past at 100 kilometres an hour, you might explore lives left in stasis. In one building, you might find an old piano, long out of tune, standing politely as upright as ever upon a raised dais. Press a key and all you would get is a distant, flat note, heavy with dust and light in music. Another house holds an old living room, fireplace blackened and unmistakable across

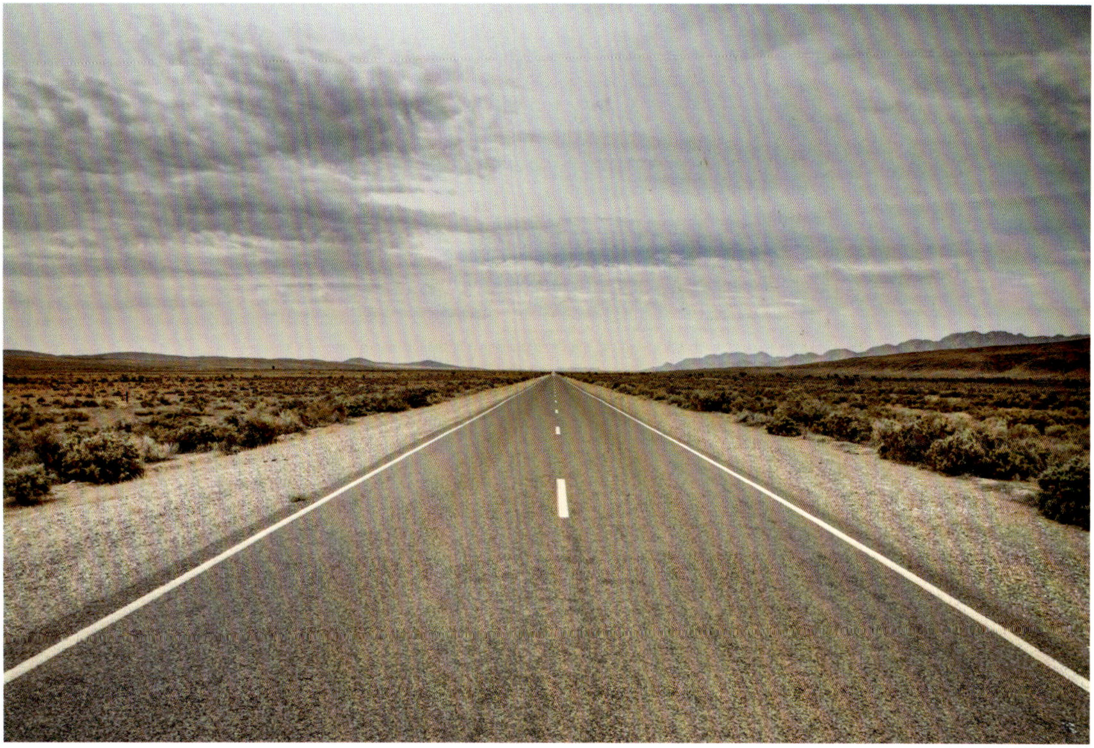

The Outback Highway.

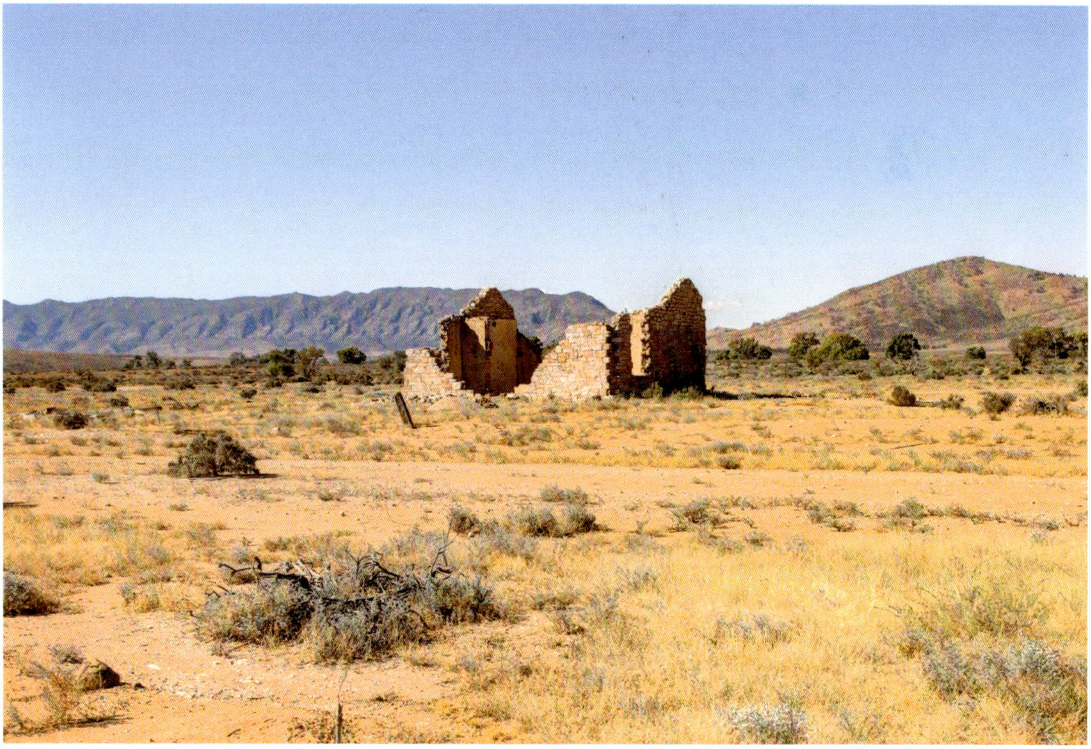

Stone ruins dot the Flinders Ranges' landscape.

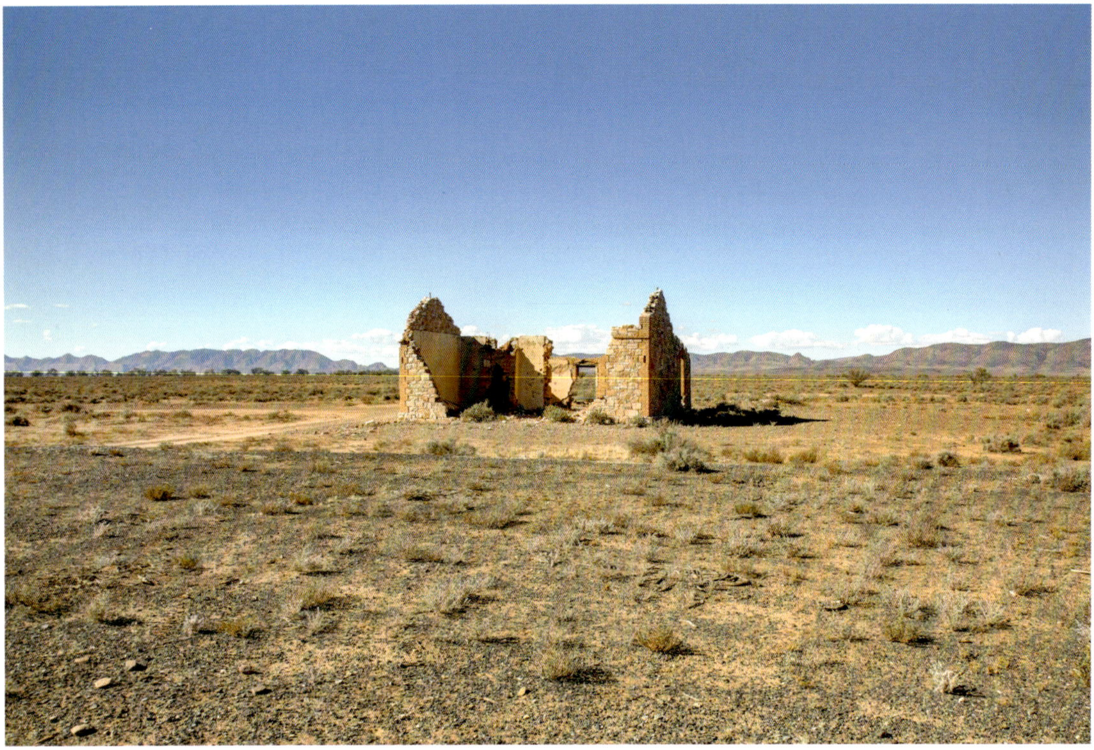

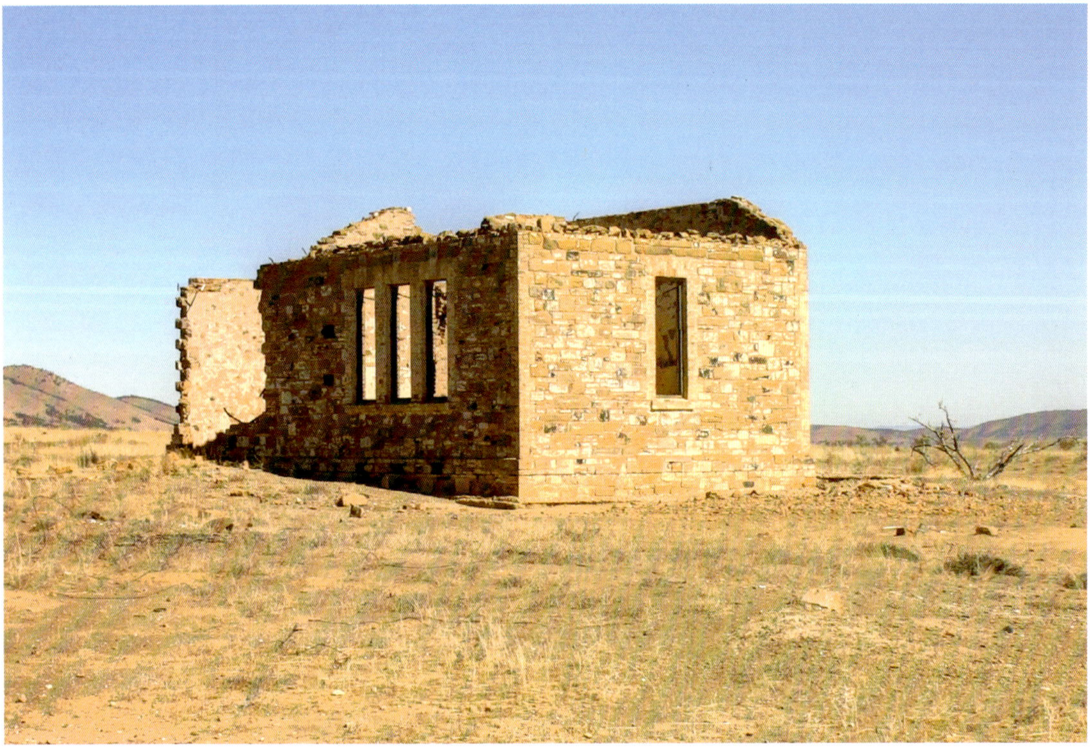

the small diagonal stretch of wall which houses it. A green chair—startling, still, in its hue among the grey and brown detritus—sits opposite it, a place where someone once sat and warmed themselves after a long day.

You might find your eye trapped by swathes of wallpaper, still intact—boasting a pattern that loses your sense of perception in it for a moment, until you blink and see the lines and cracks of the wall again. The pinkness of the faded pattern and the old, small bed frames with rusty springs tell you children, perhaps, once slept here each night.

The road continues on, the weary traveller follows the path set out for them. What else do they find?

Floors strewn with televisions and books and magazines, growing damp and mouldy—vestiges of entertainment now slowly becoming mulch—in some. Old cricket bats and biscuit tins—indication of hobbies then and now—in others. And bones, of small animals who long ago met their fate in a darkened abandoned dwelling along a long, dry road.

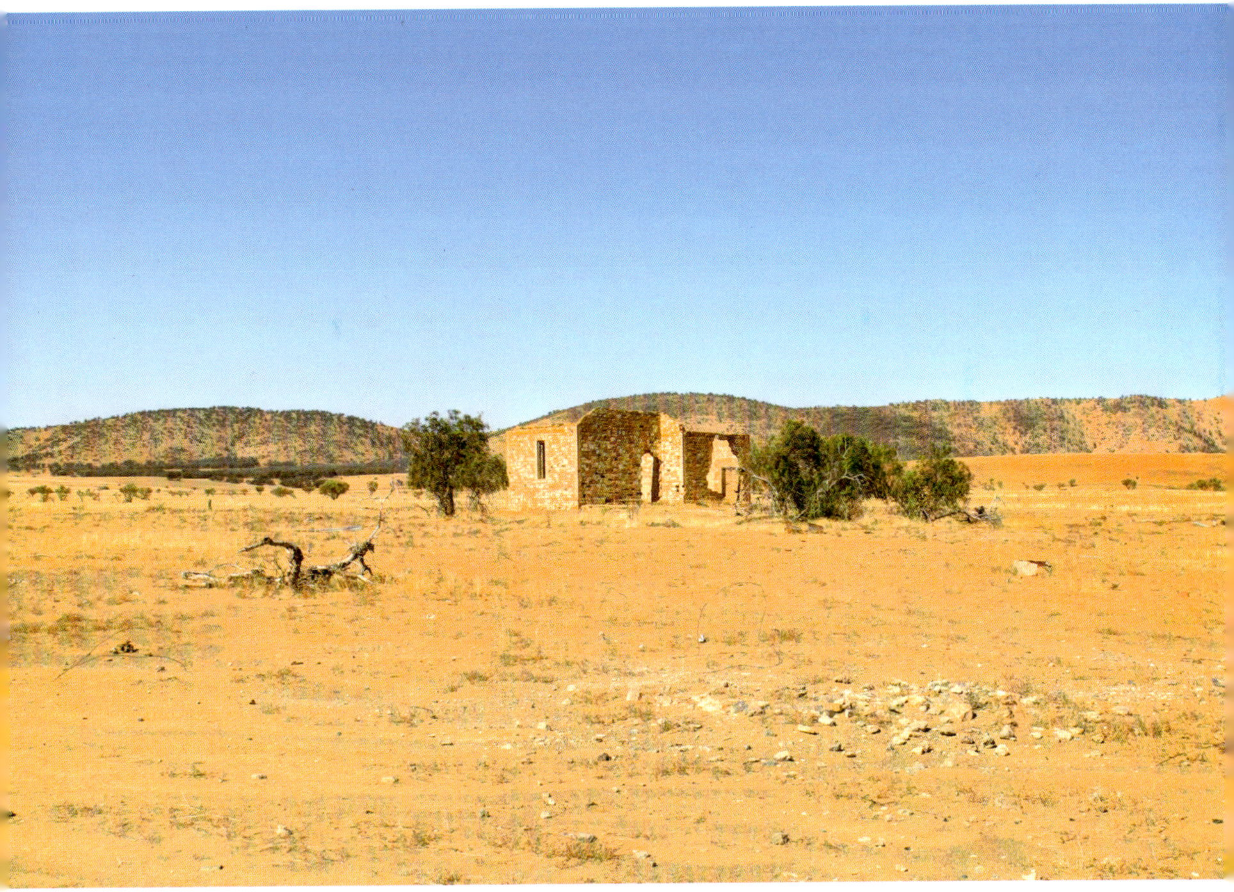

One could stand, carefully, during the daytime, between traffic, on the Outback Highway's asphalt itself, gazing towards its end. The vanishing point: is this where all the past resides now? Have the ghosts slowly and solemnly made their way, drawn towards the edge of the horizon—an edge that moves as a rainbow does when you try to locate its tether point. The ghosts of the past feel bound to this experience, lonely roads and vanishing horizons, houses on hills crumbling to the wind. They move toward a horizon point that never eventuates: onward.

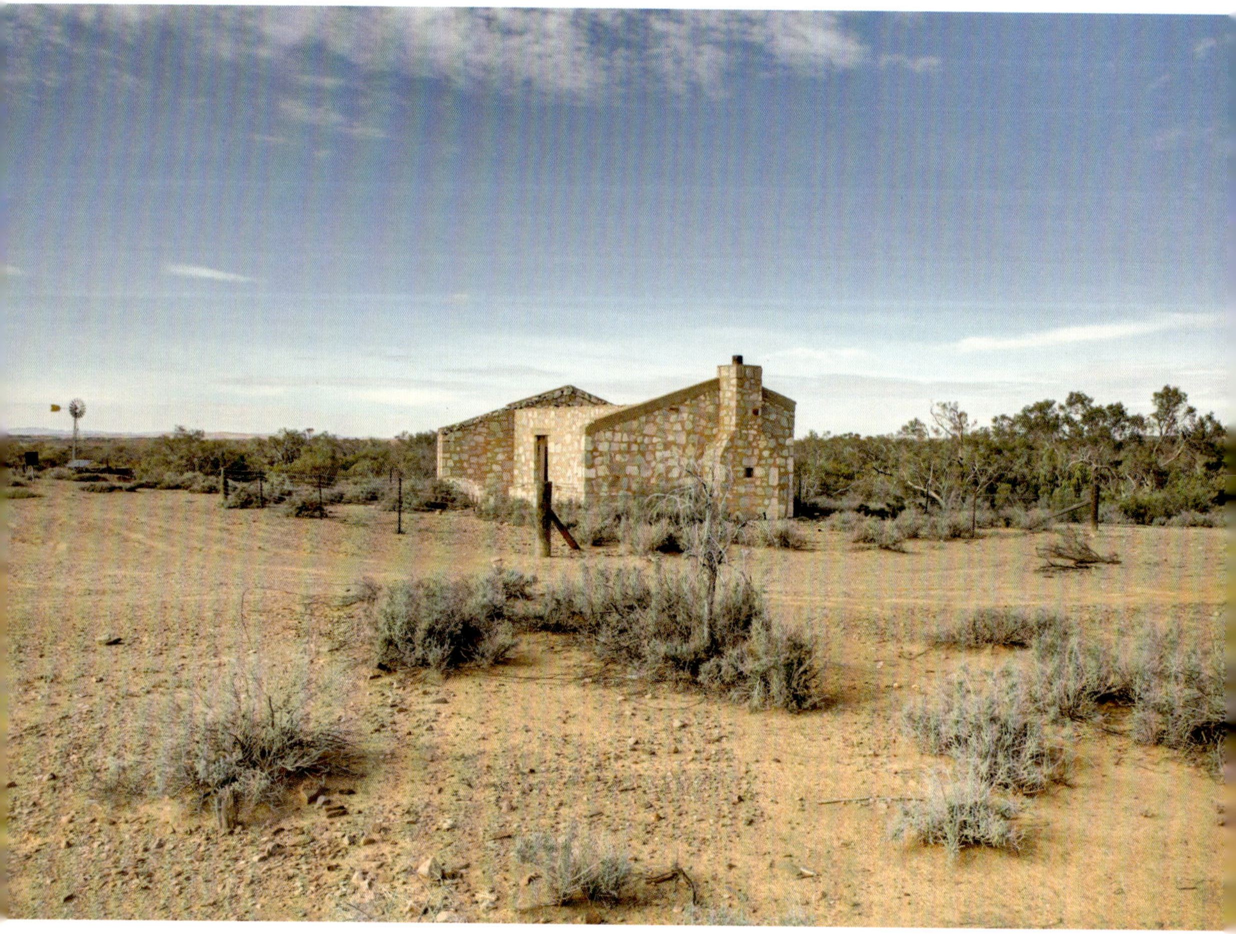

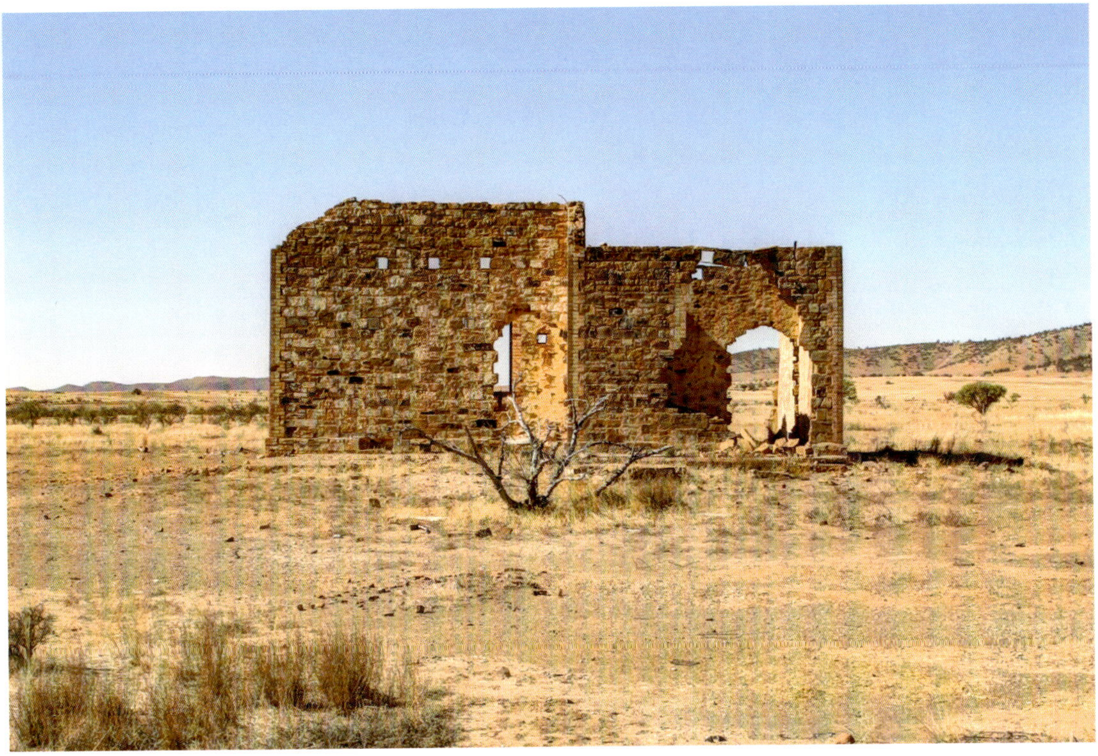

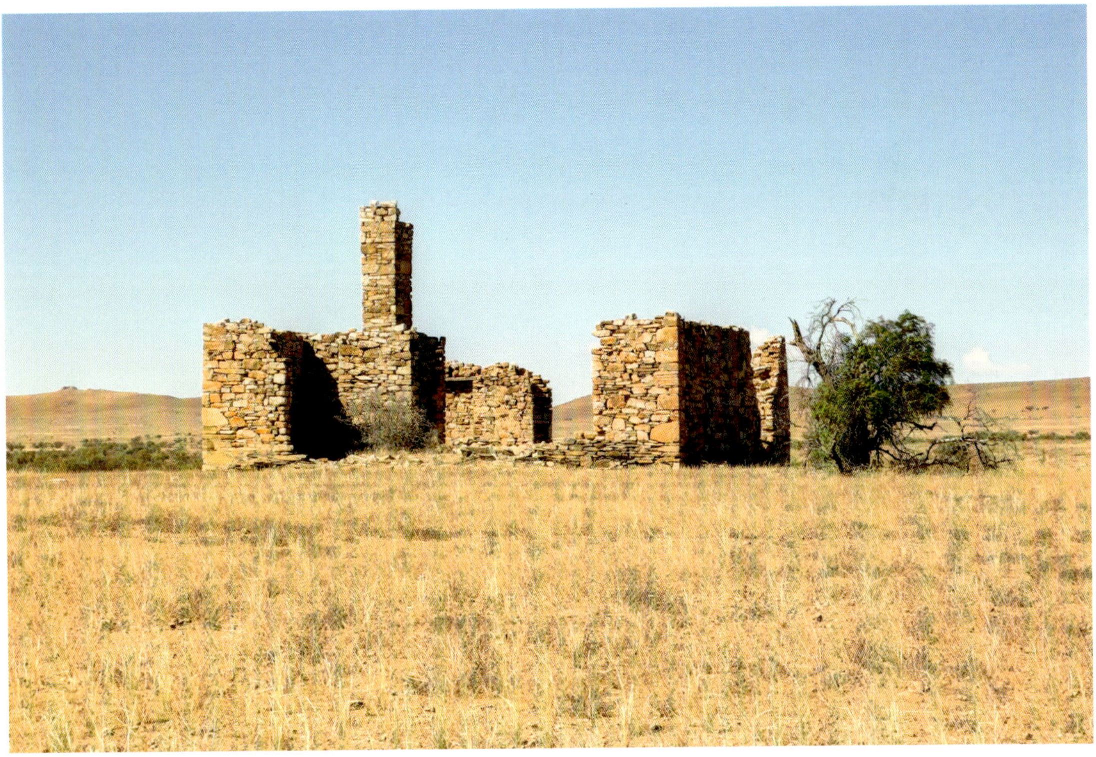

10

OUTBACK CEMETERIES

As humans trying to make sense of something non-reconcilable, we tend to think of death as fertile, in its way: bodies feeding the moss and the worms, grass and flowers lushly populating graves tended to by the bereaved. It gives us a little meaning to allocate to the meaningless. We think of those left behind as bringing life, water, and warmth to a place of greyness, and of the cemeteries resting in serenity in their absence. Sleeping, while roots grow down and the critters buried in the first layer of dirt are busy, little proxies for their sleeping humans.

But some cemeteries, like many in the outback of South Australia, are dry and arid, with no spare resources being cultivated by thirsty dirt to give moss or worms life. These places are small, generally, with a feeling of randomness to their locations: a smattering of graves, off the beaten track for any regular visitors or passers-through. These few souls rest together, often next to highways, only disturbed by truck gear noises, cicadas yelling, and rain sometimes begrudgingly hammering down on the concrete. It is peace, of a sort, if peace can be found in a 3 by 3-metre square of red dust.

These are perhaps the places where ghosts of the past are closest to the veil. Just beyond the gate. The final resting places of humans often have a hushed and respectful silence—here, the wind howls across the flat in a way that does not heed anything. Perhaps the ghosts themselves are in the howl, lonely and voicing their displeasure about this solitary location, not often mourned.

The flatness of the ground at this cemetery renders the low fence seemingly useless to the eye, more of a sculptural installation than a preventative measure. Graves made of sandstone are pale against the ruddy bushes and dirt, a landscape of surprisingly dark hue when looked at from afar. From a distance, the graves stand out whitely as if marble. Close up, one can see the years of wind and dust storms sticking to them, like imprints of the past. Each grave tells a story, and each story ends here—in the Outback Cemetery, where bones come to sleep.

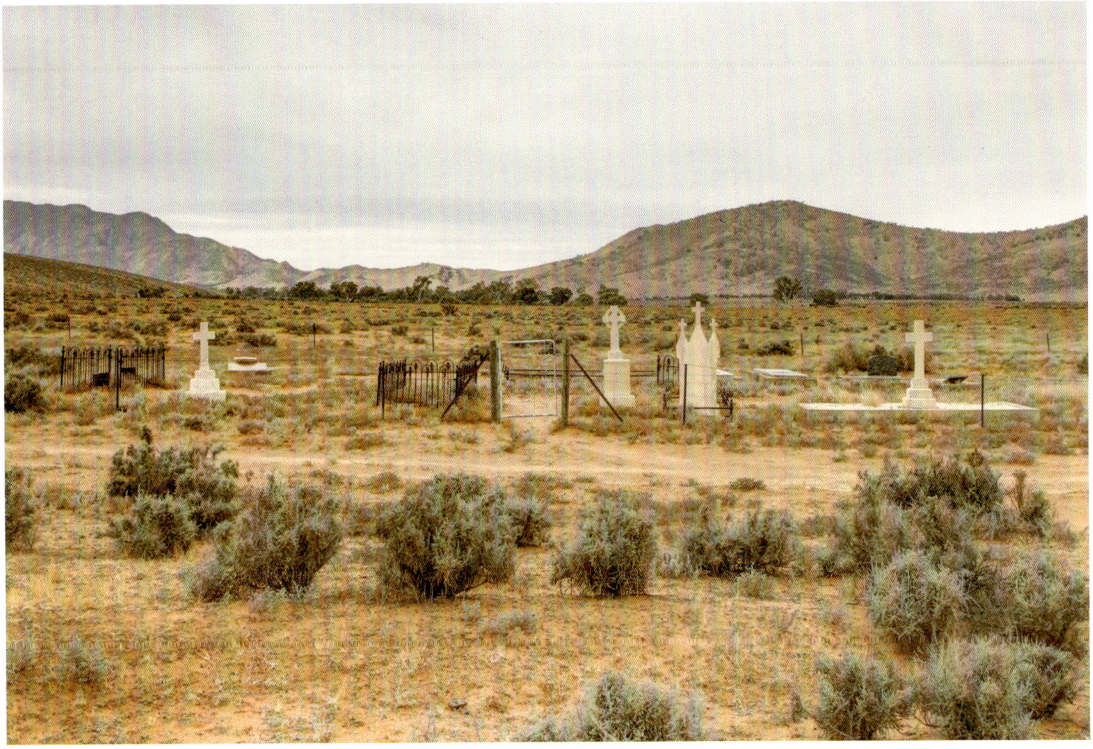

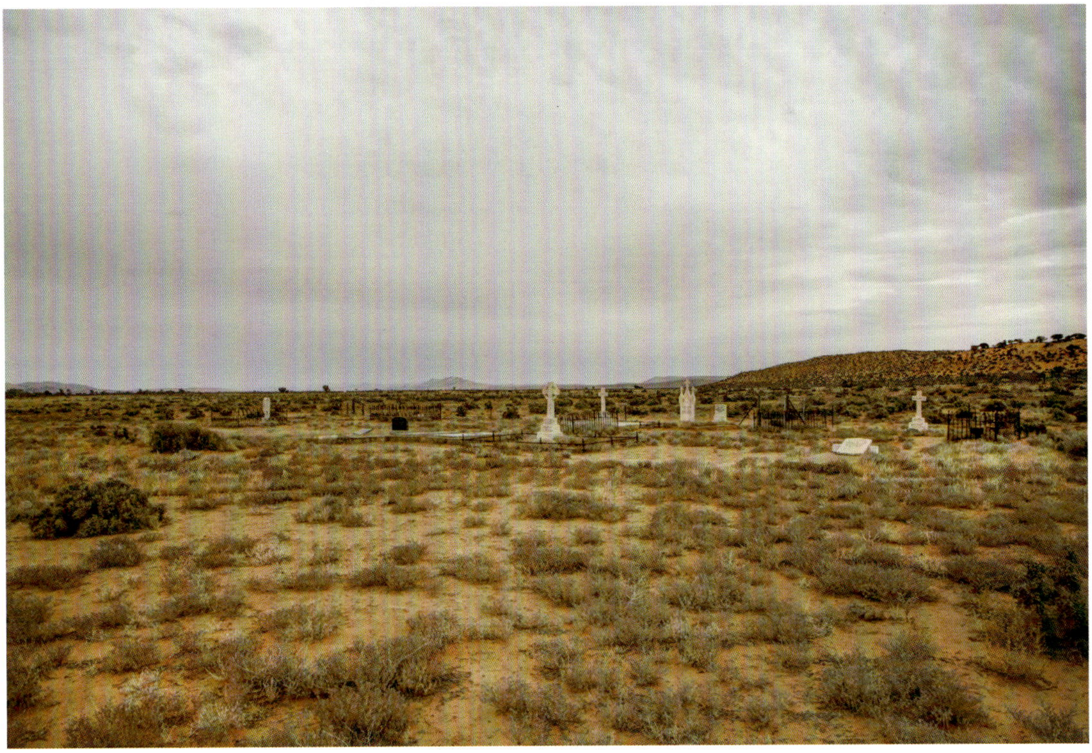

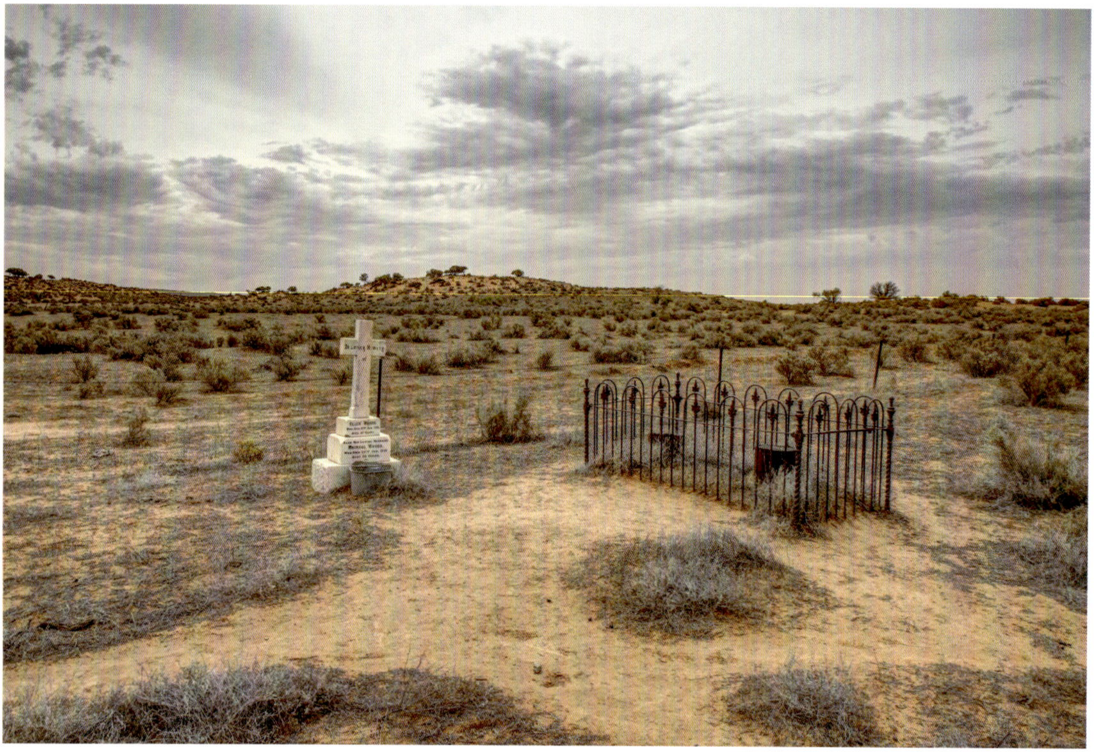

The stories, however, are not always put into physical words. Not every soul resting here has a marked grave, a headstone with five to eight words and some numbers, summing up in a few figures what took twenty or fifty or ninety years to unfold. 'Always loved and never forgotten', 'Beloved wife to Moira and father to Jane'. Small fragments of words mark a grave as someone who lived and someone who was loved.

But many of the graves here do not have these. Perhaps they once did, stones lovingly picked out by family and laid respectfully into the ground. Flowers once were laid on the white stone. The flowers would not last long, though, the sun baking them from colourful to brown quickly. And weather—years of harsh wind and the alternating forces of sun and wind—has carried off the letters and figures from some headstones, often obscuring them to make them unreadable. Some of these graves, and the people resting in them, are marked only by the sun casting shadows as it moves throughout the day. And days pass slowly here.

This place is mossless and unfrequented. This place is quiet but loud, all at the same time. The eeriness abounds and the loneliness is more potent than most other cemeteries. Nobody is gathering to discuss the people buried here, whoever they were, and whichever way their ancestral tendrils unfold. Unmarked graves are the territory, mostly, of ghosts, and these ghosts must be restless.

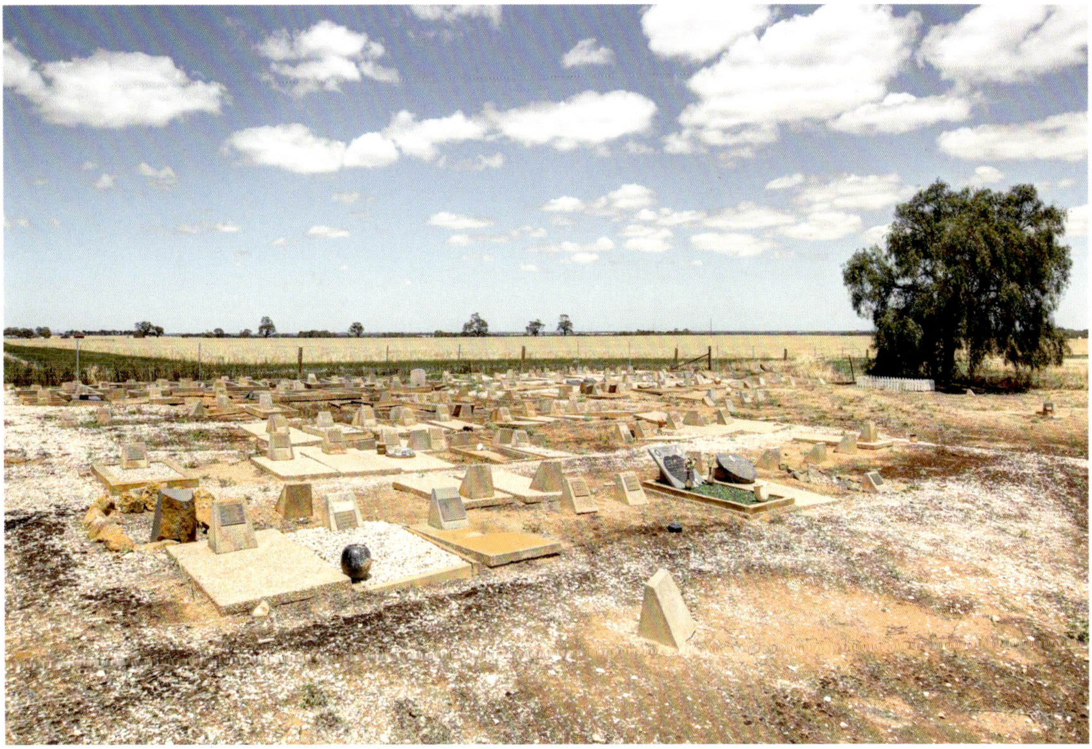

The final resting place for over 200 beloved pets, Atkinsons Cemetery is a touching rural space where pet owners once paid respects to their furry and feathered friends long since passed. Established in 1972 with a cost of up to $400 a plot (and an optional coffin and burial service), the forgotten graveyard was purchased in 2010 and will form a small piece of what is to set become a new housing development.

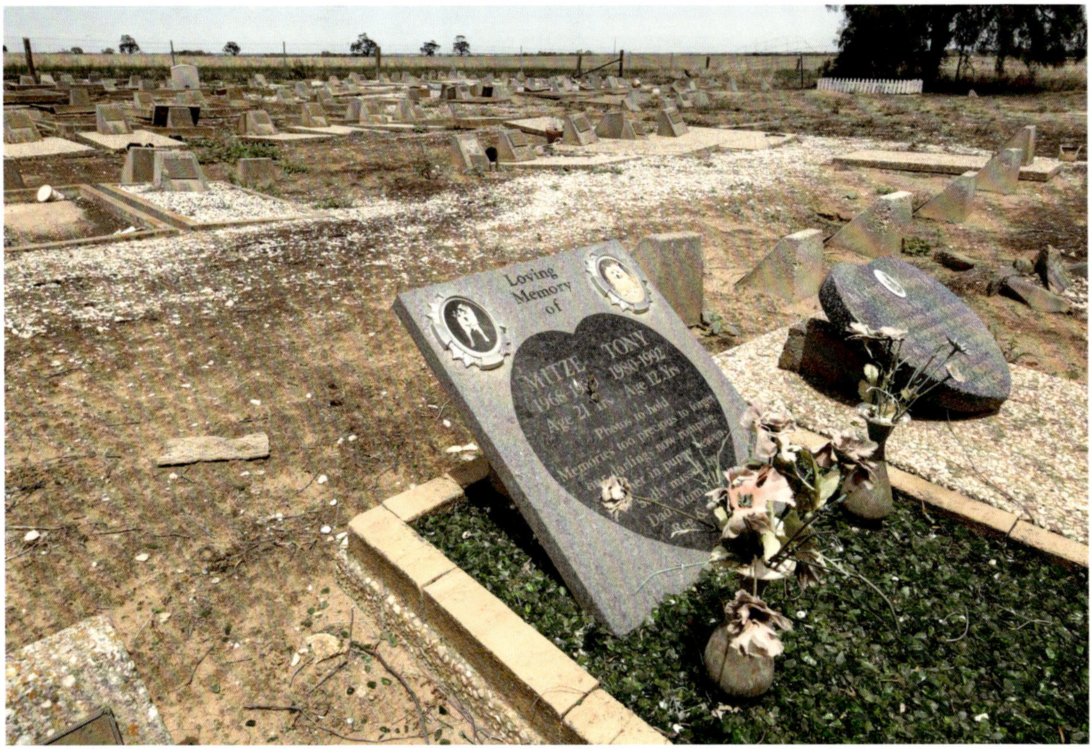

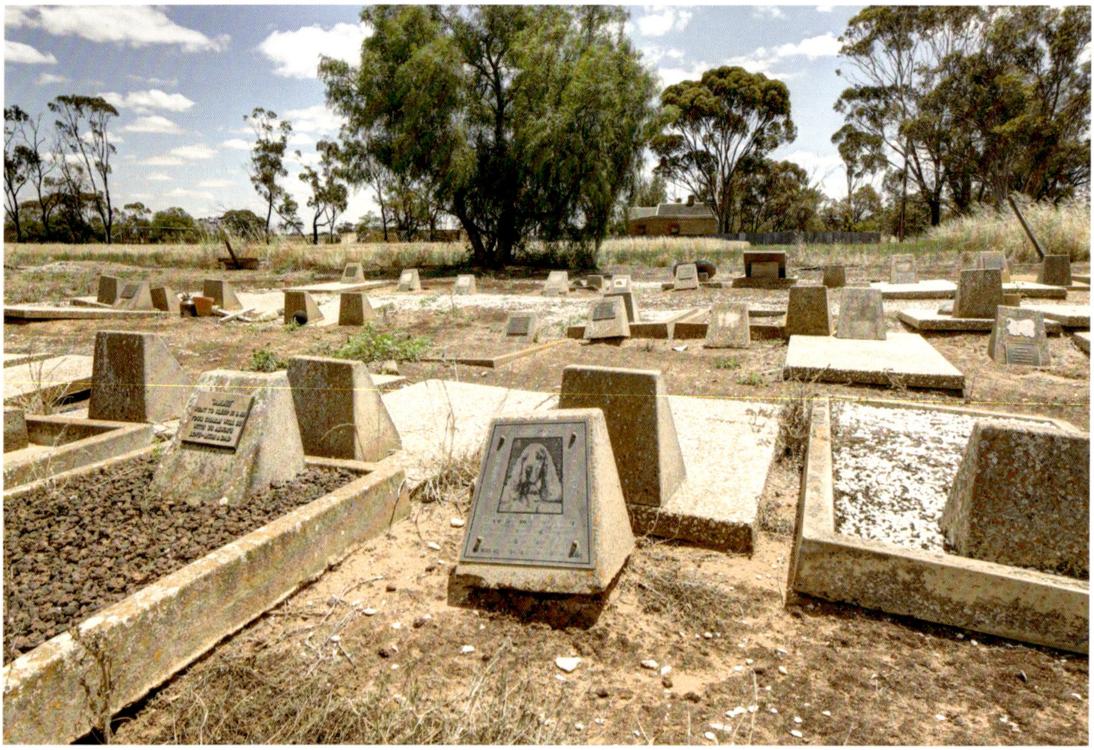

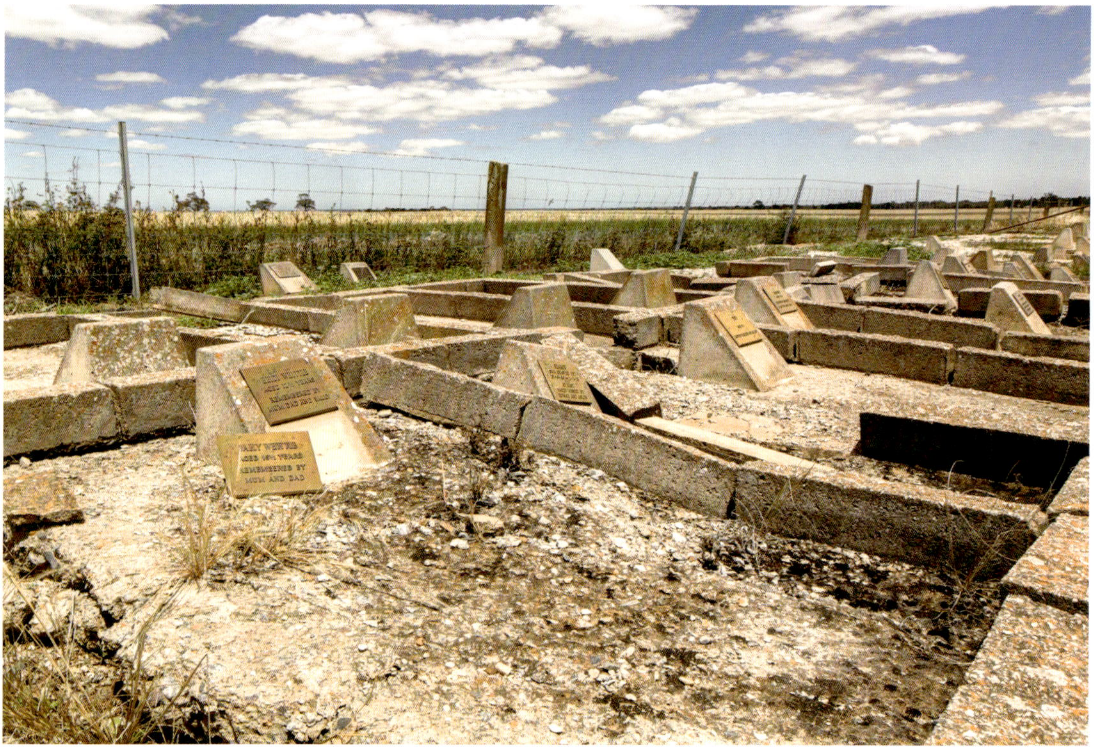
REMEMBERED BY
MUM AND DAD

11

FARINA GHOST TOWN

Farina—formerly known as Farina Town, and originally called The Gums, or Government Gums—most likely is not a town with which many people are familiar. It is a near certainty that you will not come across many, if any, who will tell you about a childhood spent growing up within the few sparse square kilometres that circle this deserted township.

And yet, the camping ground and walking trails are open 365 days a year. Its dilapidated remains sit on the edge of the dusty Outback Highway, north of Lyndhurst by 26 kilometres—with an official population of zero, and marked as "ruins" on any map. The town sits within the Lake Eyre Basin and, as well, on the old alignment of the Ghan railway.

Settled in 1878 by farmers and built on the promise of bountiful wheat and barley production ('Farina' is the Italian word for flour), silver and copper mines were also dug in the surrounding areas. Farina was utilised as a trucking yard for livestock travelling down the Birdsville Track, and the town was the area's railhead until 1884. However, the town became prey to the region's poor agricultural conditions. A harsh desert climate meant that most of the land—contrary to the optimistic farm hopes—was unworkable.

Pre-abandonment, in the late 1800s, the town peaked at a population of 600. There were five blacksmiths, two hotels, two breweries, a bakery, a bank, a church, a school, a brothel. There were metal and sheep wranglers, publicans, bakers and drinkers. Prayers, bankers and prostitutes. All the hallmarks of a society that can keep itself running on work and play.

Farina's fate, however, was to end up—100 years later—with none of these things save sandstone ruins and the old railway water tank. Full-time life ceased. The town became totally abandoned, with no residents within the township itself at all. Ghosts moved in and dust storms blew silently, with no one to hear them roar.

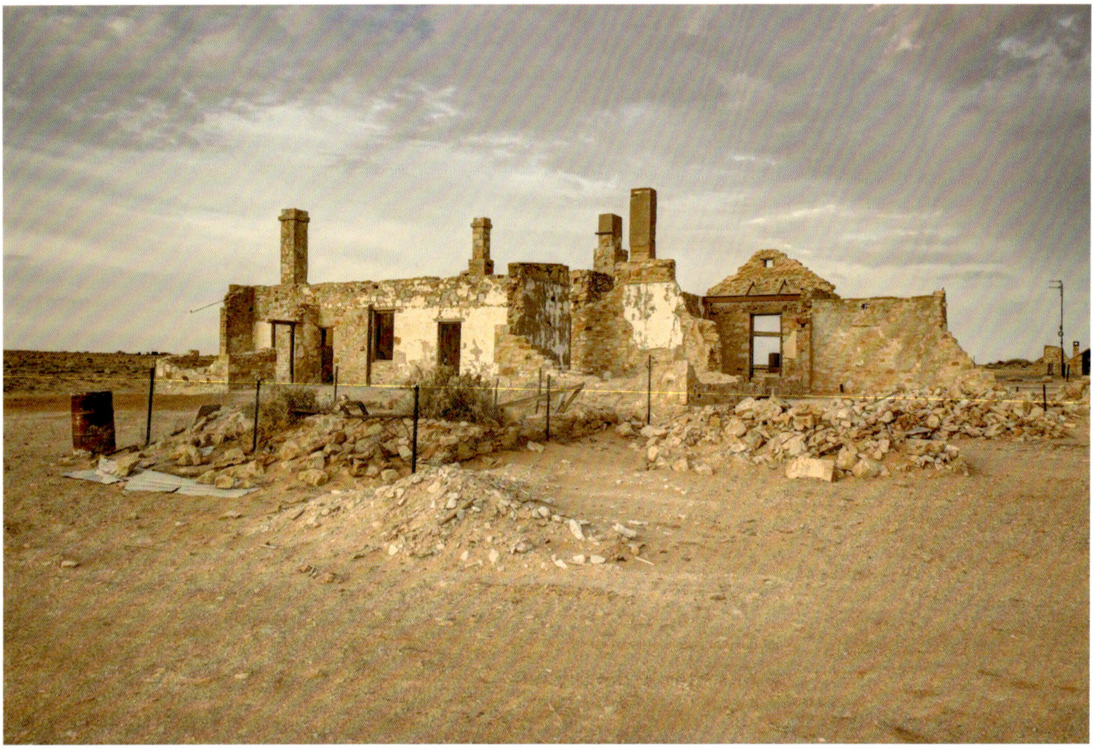

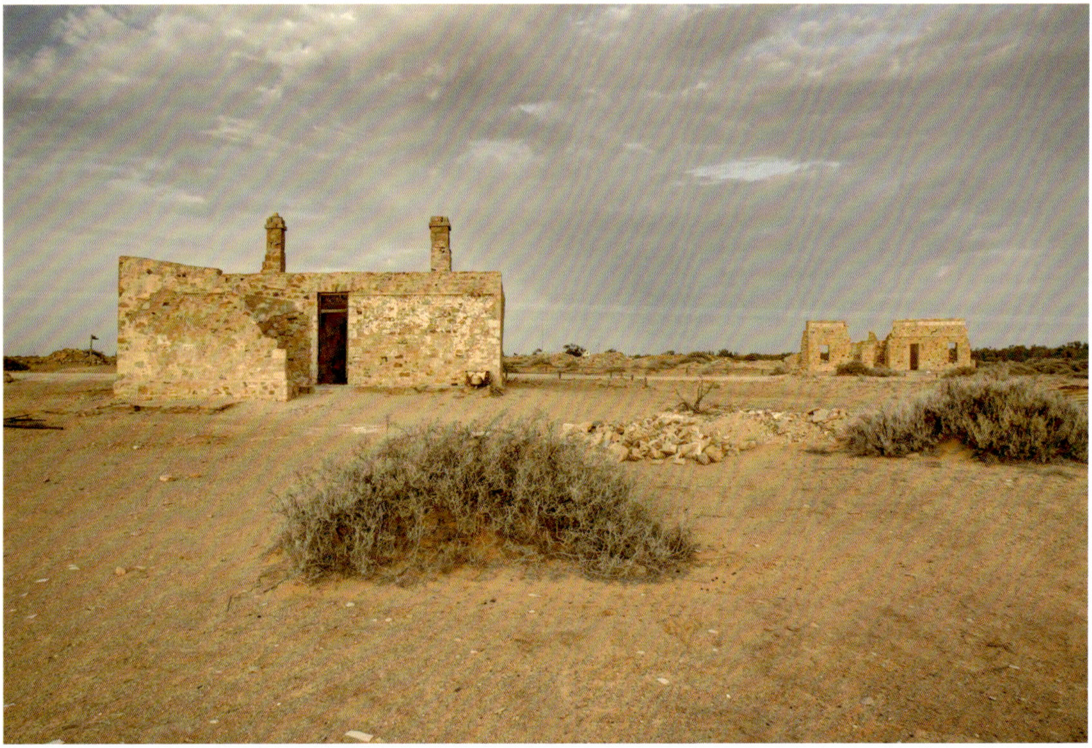

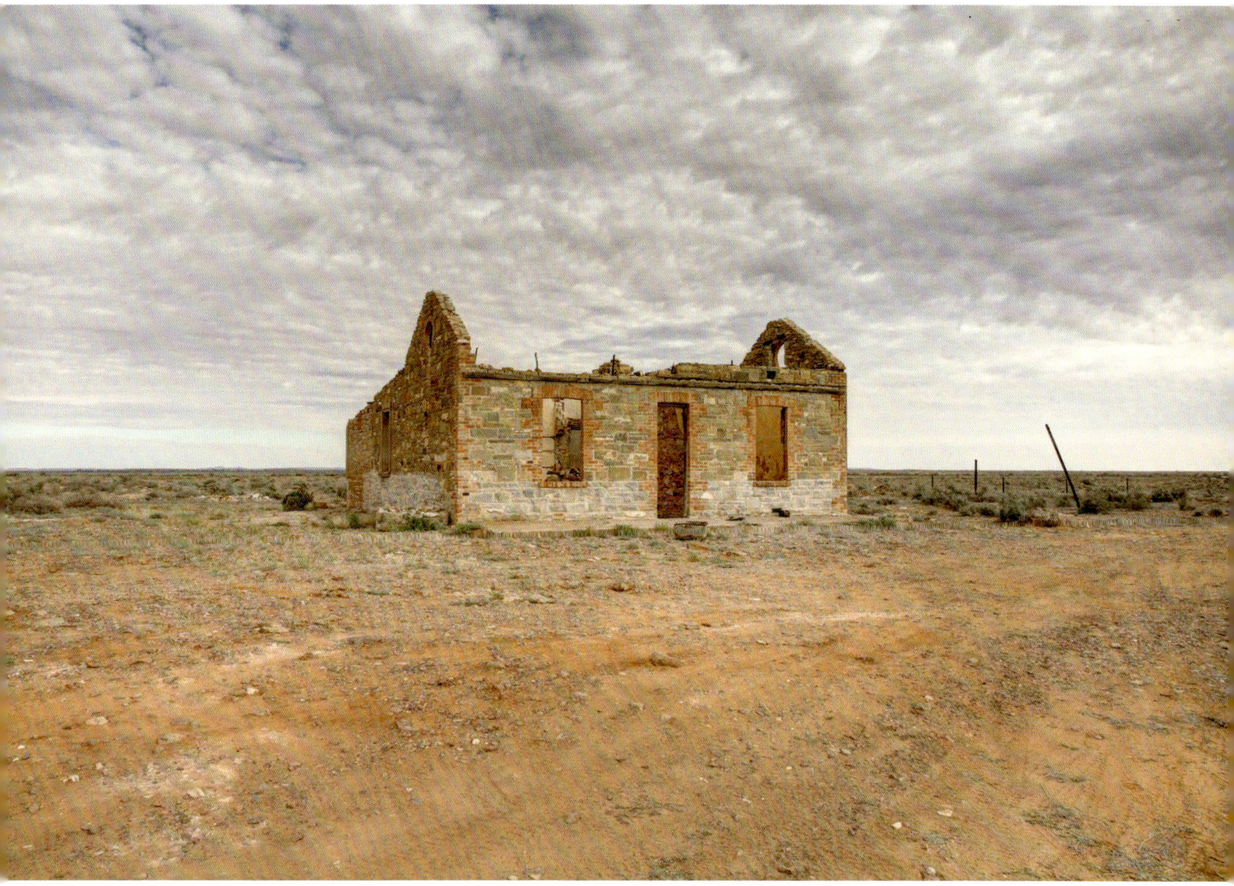

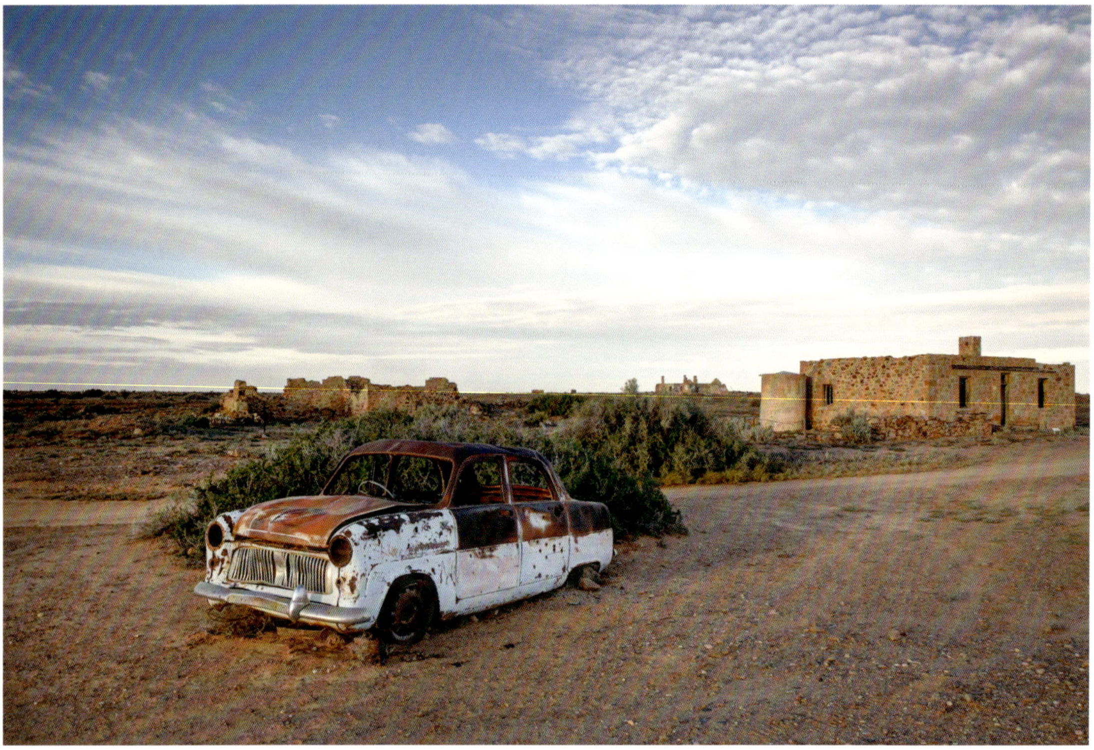

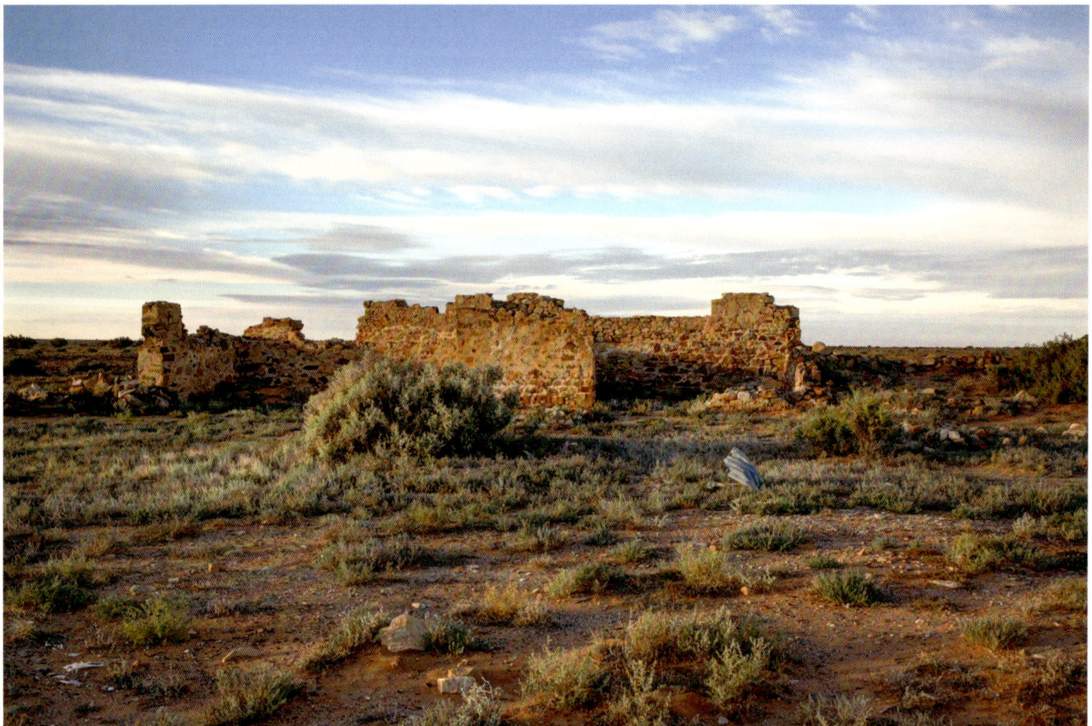

But now, surprisingly, there is life. There exists a small but very dedicated group of volunteers devoted to bringing Farina back from the brink of extinction—The Farina Restoration Group, founded in 2008. The group operates between May and July each year, running a works program fuelled by the passions of the couple who own Farina Station and a tour guide who was familiar with the town.

People travel to Farina each year to see the bones of the place and how they are being replenished; a pilgrimage, attracting more and more visitors each time. The group of volunteers draws many helpers, bringing a tiny amount of life back into the red, dusty ruins of a place ghostly in its reputation, but each year, slightly less ghostly in its demeanour. Carpenters and stonemasons and builders all lend their expertise. Informational signs are placed all around the town, optimistically informing the public about the ongoing project and the town's history.

But the pride and joy of Farina, with its new life breathed into it, is the bakery. Lovingly rebuilt around an underground scotch oven, it is now fully operational, churning out slices, cream buns, and loaves of bread during the winter months. The smells permeate a quiet town, suddenly invoking strong feelings of lives once lived. The sandstone must relish in the scent of fresh bread once more being blown through it.

While there are no current residents within the town itself, the nearest ones are not that far: Farina Station is nearby and populated. Life creeps back, and the fumes of fresh bread smell of hope. Perhaps Farina will one day host full-time locals once more, and the ghosts will move on to another town.

If you are driving near Lyndhurst in the winter, along the Outback Highway, and you see a sign that says "Bakery Baking Today" under the turn-off to Farina, stop off. You might not be the only one.

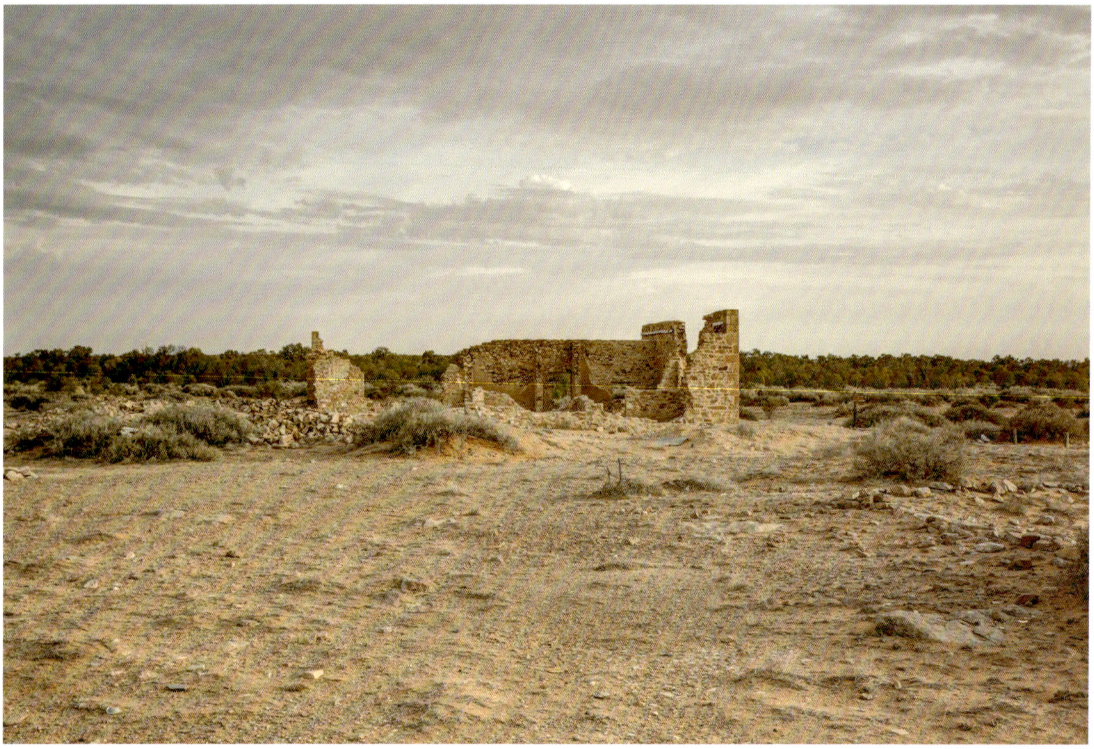

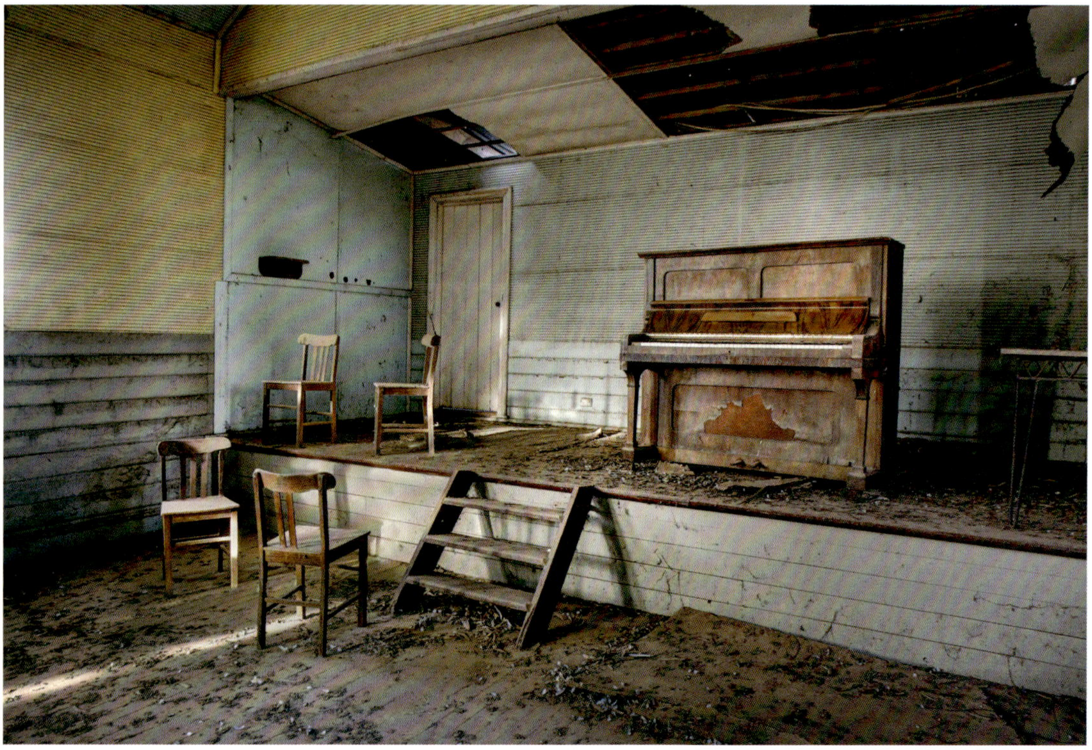

A former community hall in the state's mid-north.

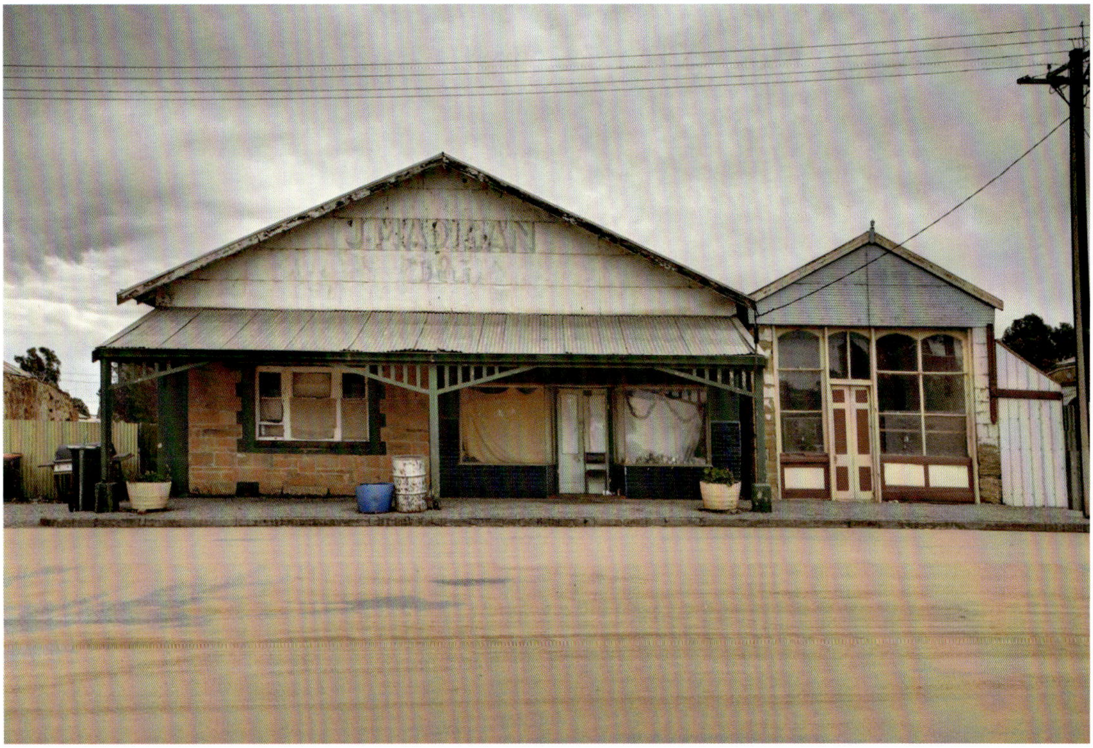

Terowie (the Aboriginal word for 'hidden waterhole') is a semi-abandoned township in the state's mid-north. The town's historical period charm and atmosphere have become a draw card for filmmakers.

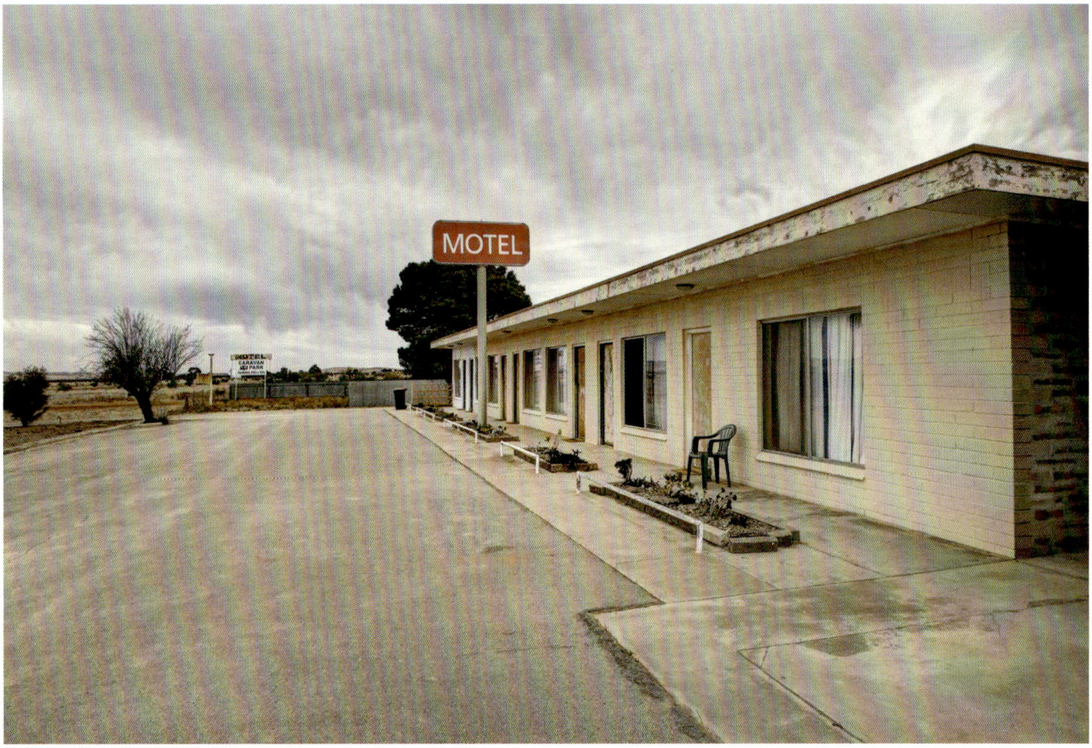

A moody-looking motel at Terowie's entrance.

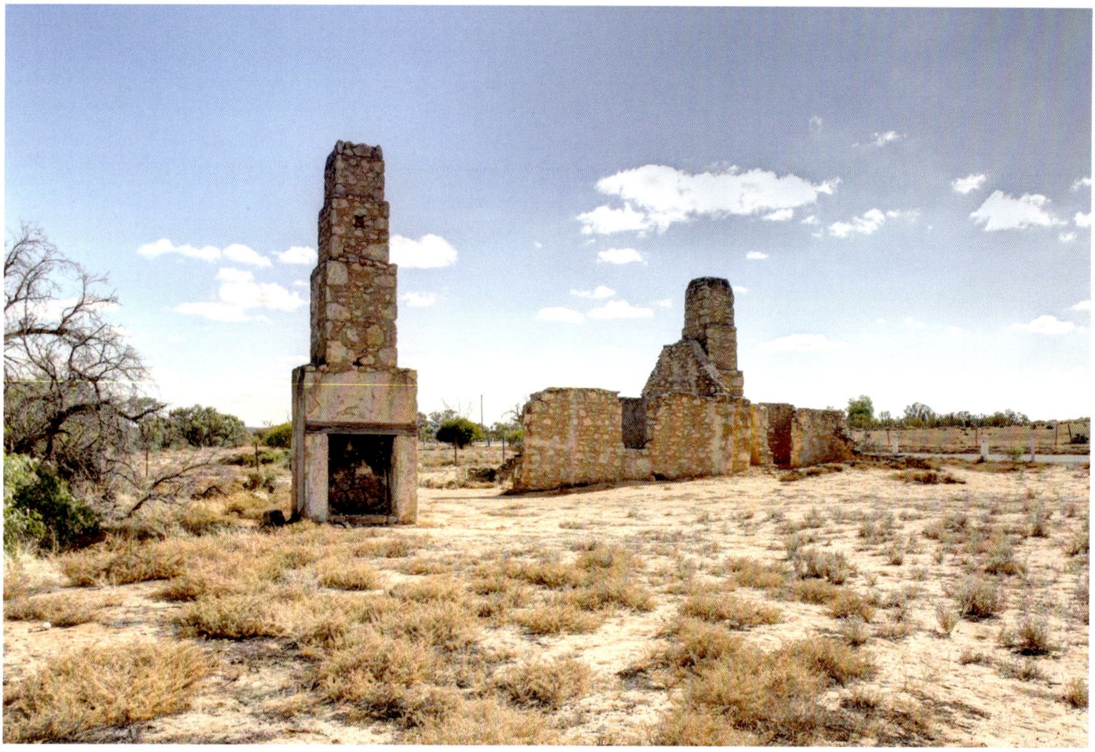

Ruins of the former Lake Bonney Hotel. The eleven-room structure opened in 1859 and closed in 1907.

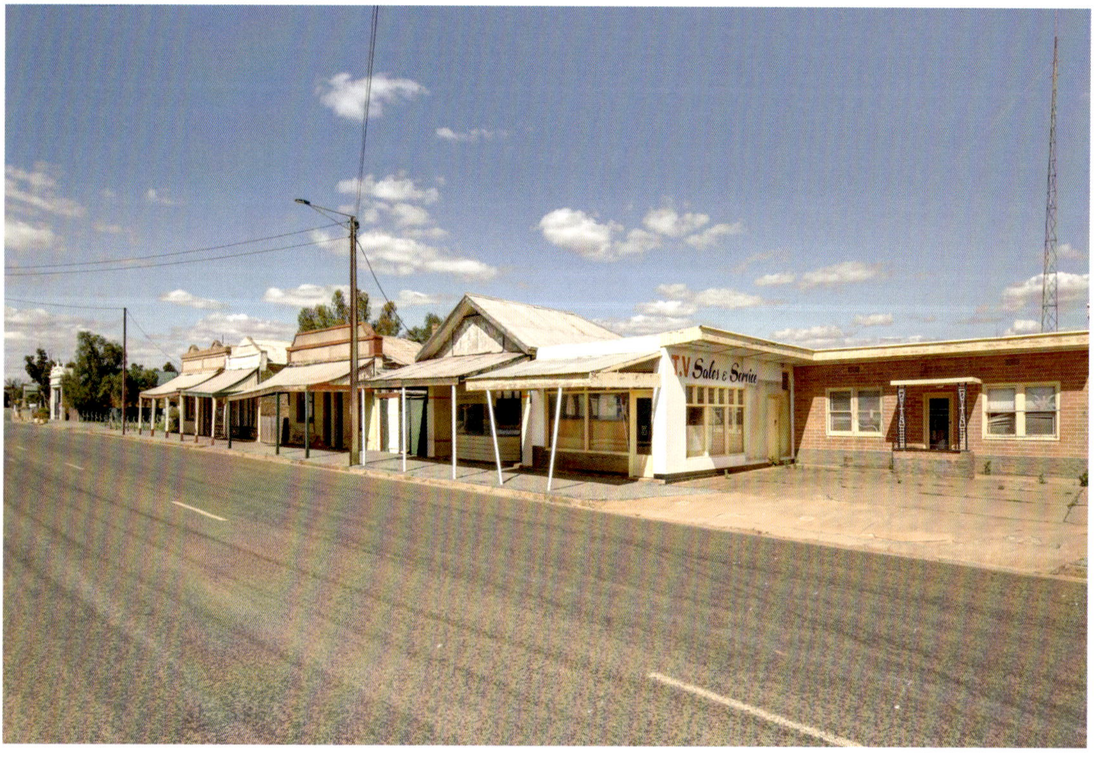

The township of Terowie hasn't changed much over the years. The original shop fronts add a vintage quality to the main street.

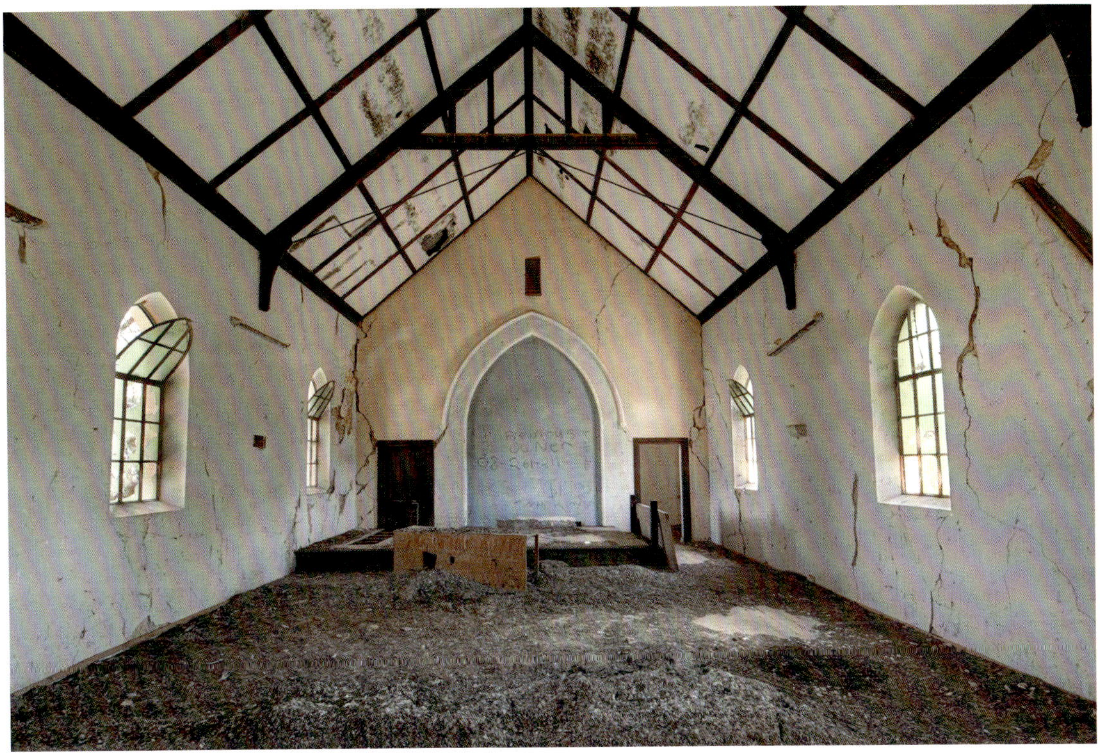

A Congregational Church interior littered with bird faeces.

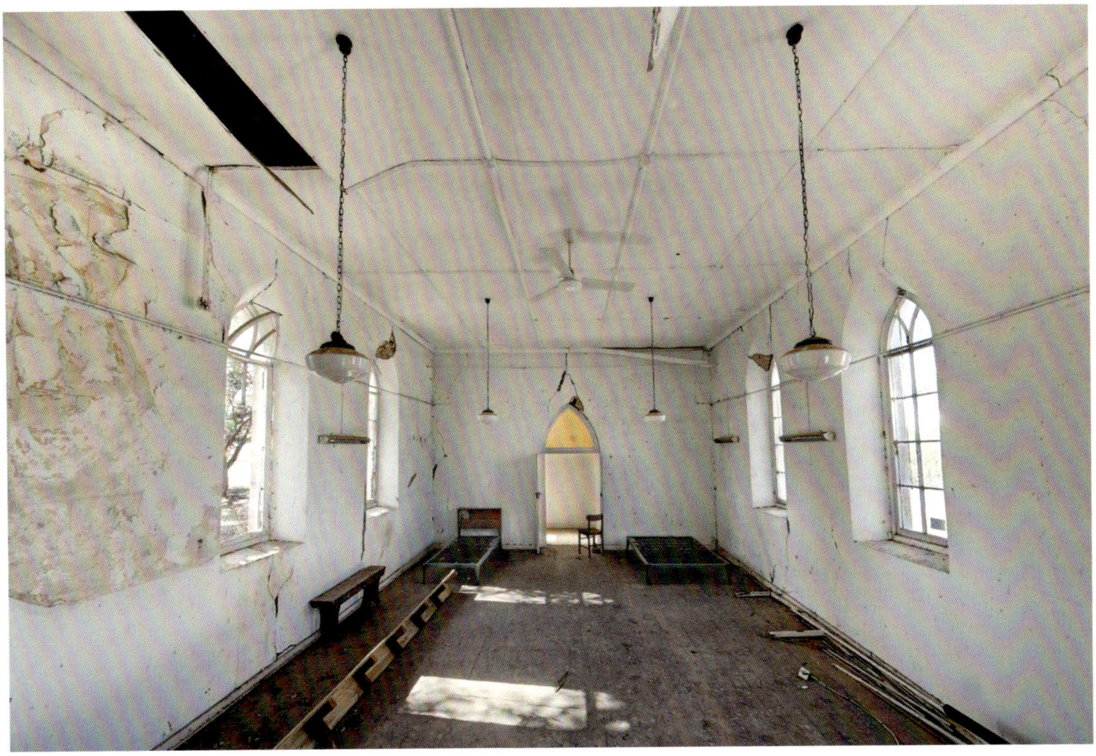

Not much remains of the church's original interior apart from its school house pendant lights and a handful of pews.

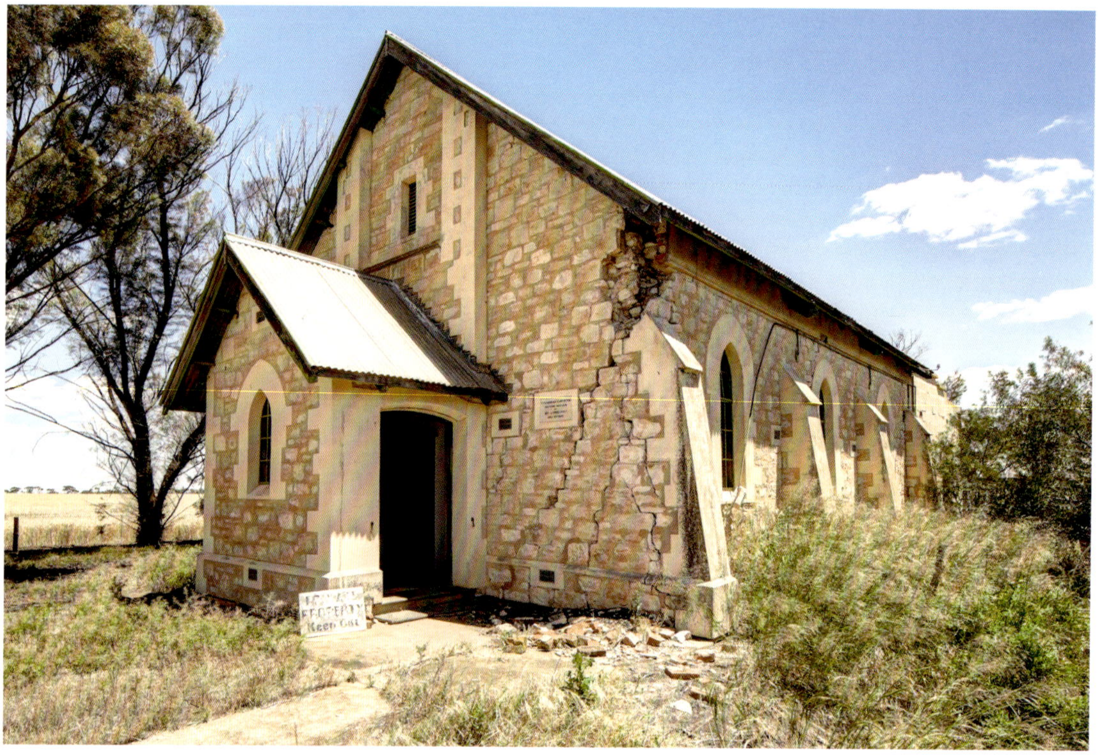

A forgotten church in the Alma region. Built in 1865, the dilapidated structure is now home to pigeons and owls.

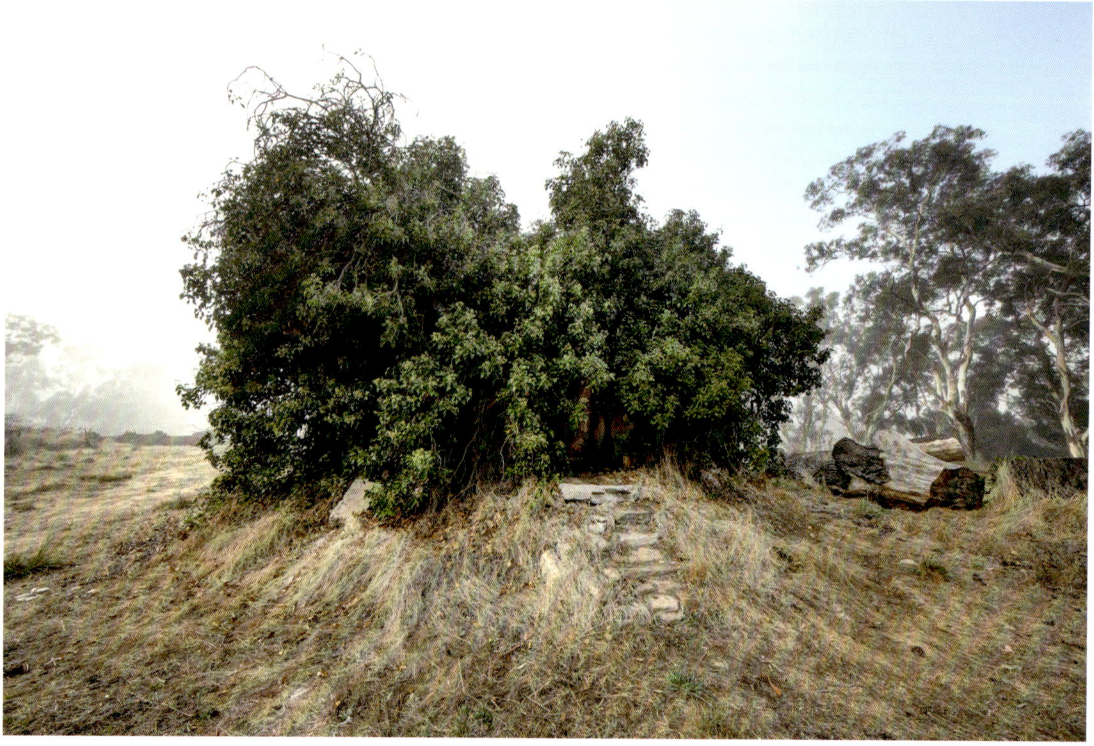

The remains of this former church are barely visible under years of overgrowth.

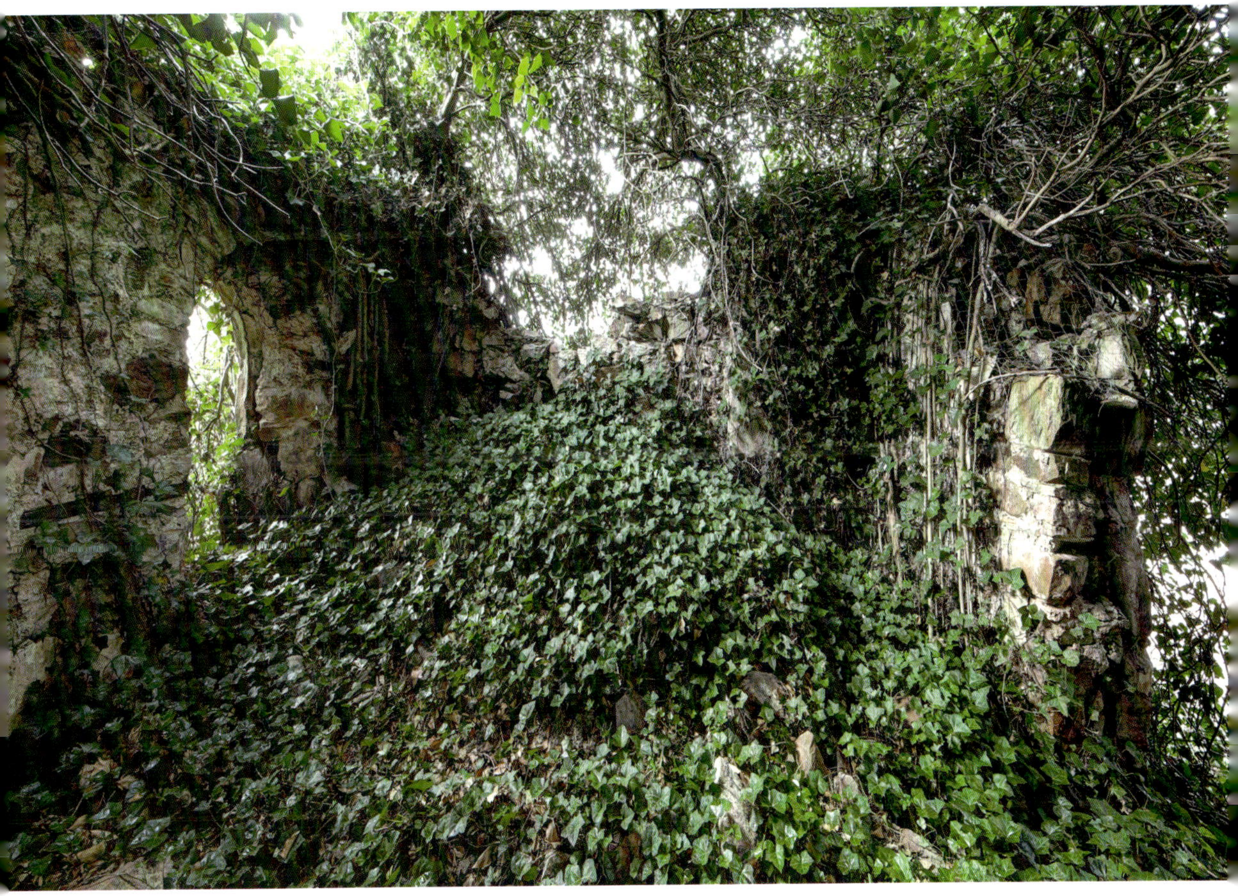

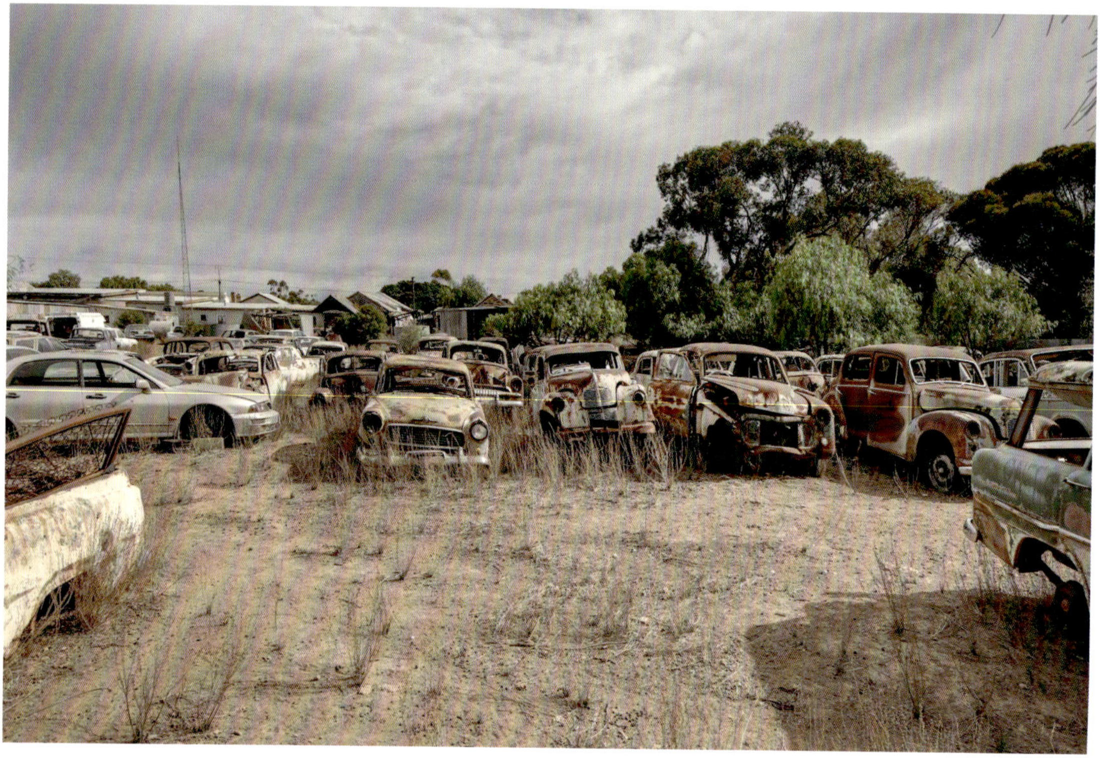

A car graveyard in Terowie.

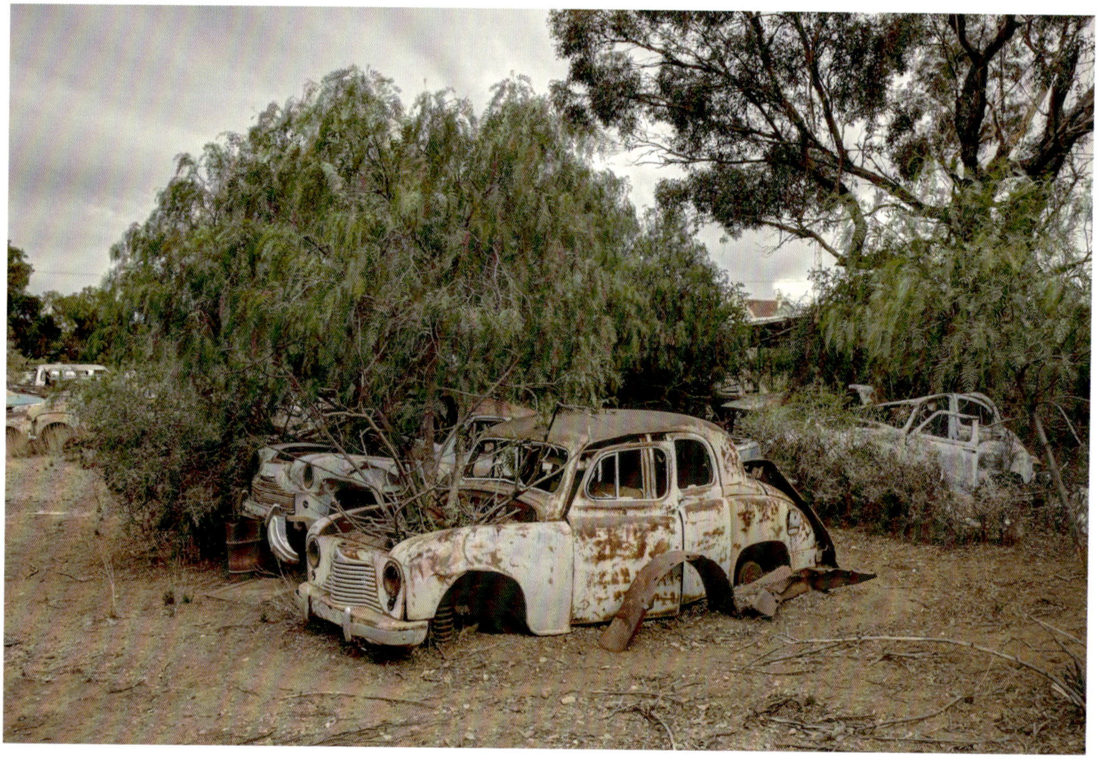

Abandoned cars are a common sight all over Australia.

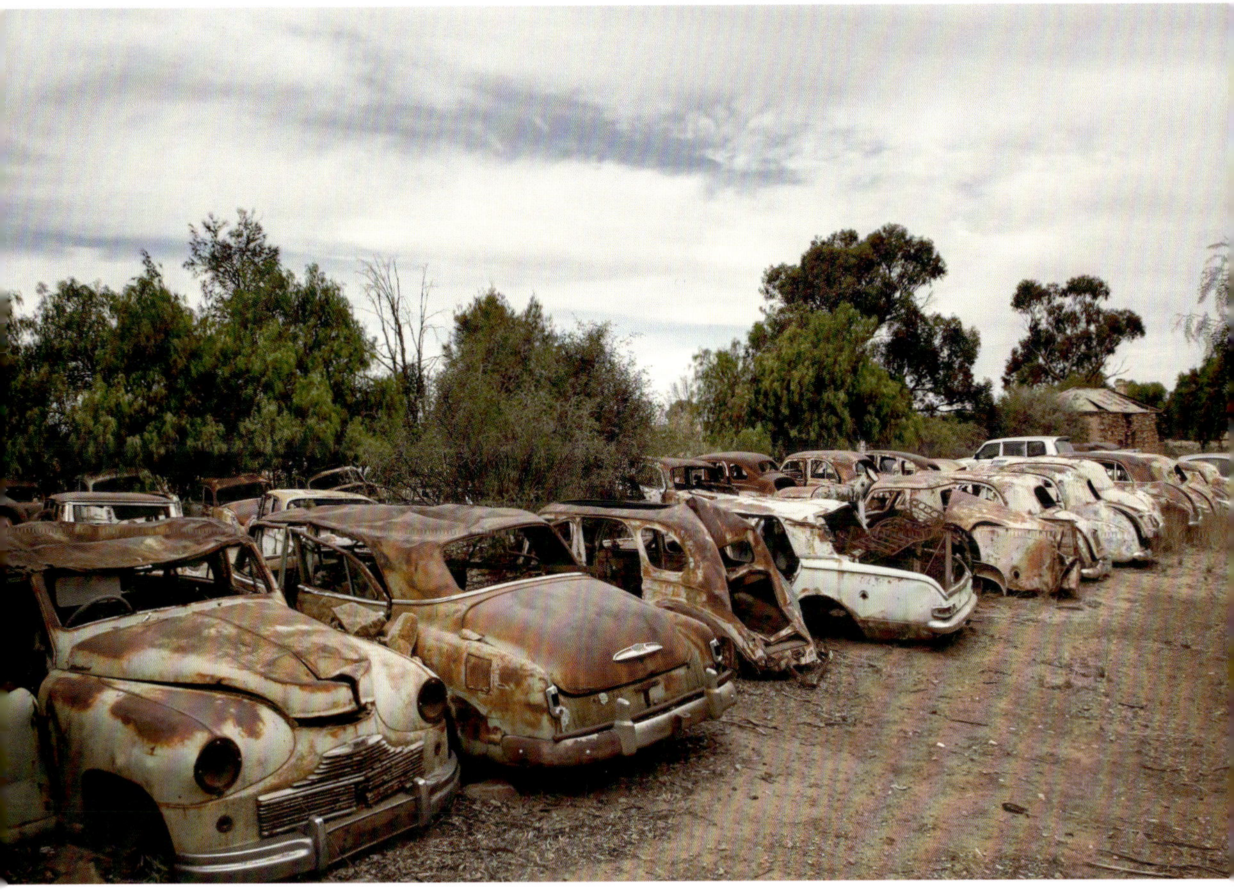

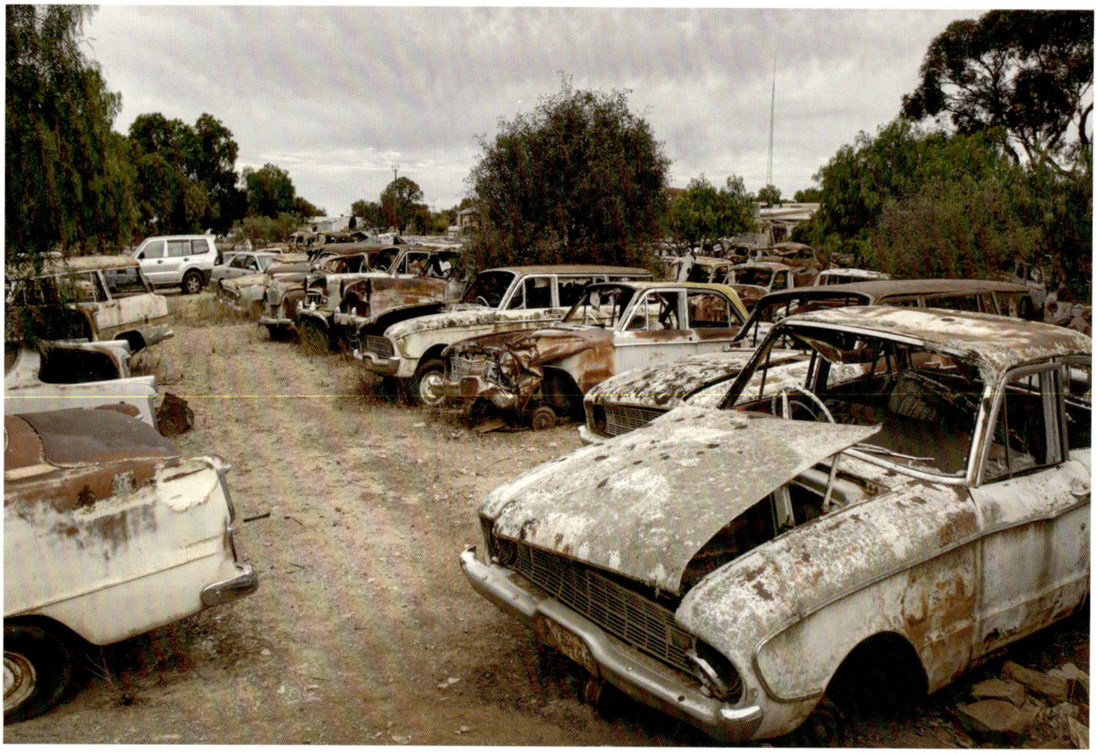

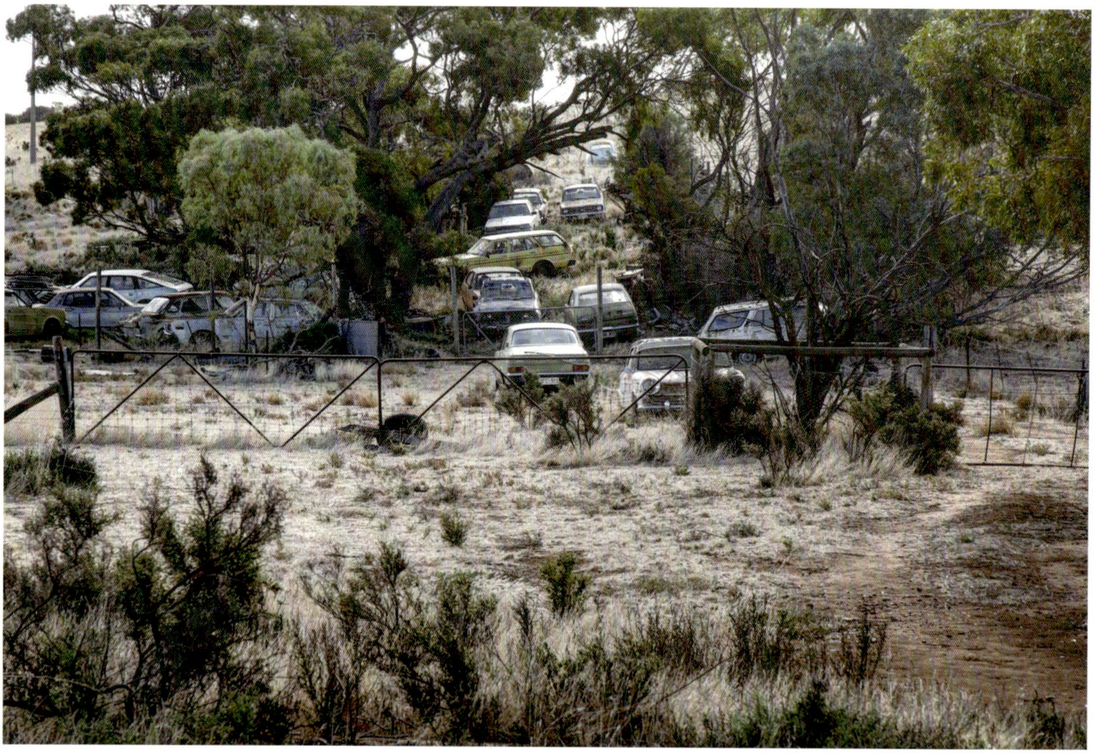

Back paddocks on rural properties sometimes become the final resting place for generations of discarded cars.